Hanky Panky

AN INTIMATE HISTORY OF THE HANDKERCHIEF

Helen Gustafson

PHOTOGRAPHY BY JONATHAN CHESTER

TEN SPEED PRESS
BERKELEY / TORONTO

Ten Speed Press
P.O. Box 7123
Berkeley, California 94707
www.tenspeed.com

Distributed in Australia by Simon and Schuster Australia, in Canada by Ten Speed Press Canada,
in New Zealand by Southern Publishers Group, in South Africa by Real Books, in Southeast Asia
by Berkeley Books, and in the United Kingdom and Europe by Airlift Book Company.

Cover and Interior Design by Stefanie Hermsdorf

Library of Congress Cataloging-in-Publication Data

Gustafson, Helen.
Hanky panky : an intimate history of the handkerchief / by Helen Gustafson.
p. cm.
ISBN 1-58008-418-4
1. Handkerchiefs--History. 2. Handkerchiefs--United States--History.
I. Title.
GT2135 .G87 2002
391.4--dc21
2002007559

First printing, 2002

Printed in Korea

1 2 3 4 5 6 7 8 9 10 — 05 04 03 02

For Winifred Yen Wood
whose encouragement fulfills my family's credo:
Kind words can never die.

ACKNOWLEDGMENTS

I want to offer my heartfelt thanks to the following people for their marvelous contributions to this book.

Arthur Ballet

Inez Brooks-Myers *of The Oakland Museum of California*

L.L. & R.C. Buchta

Jonathan Chester

Chandra Cho

Jim Dodge

Judith Dunham

Pat Edwards

Hisako Ezzard

Antonia Fusco

Gus Gustafson

Jill Gustafson

Heather Hafleigh

Stefanie Hermsdorf

Rosalie Horsted

David Jouris

Kaethe Kliot *of Lacis, Berkeley, California*

Dorothy Laupa

Lee Ann Lyman

Joni Miller

Annie Nelson *of Ten Speed Press*

Patty Peterson

Renata Polt

Lisa Scholten

Dr. Miki Masa Shima

Toni Stimpson

Steve Walton

Todd Walton

Alice Waters

Lynn Wiener

Philip Wood

CONTENTS

FOREWORD

In August of 1998, as a curator at the South Dakota Art Museum, home of the Marghab Linen Collection, I received a call from Helen Gustafson. She was visiting from Berkeley, California, to spend the summer months on her farm in Arlington, South Dakota. She wanted to stop by the Museum to meet with me and view the Marghab handkerchiefs. We spent a delightful afternoon in the museum library discussing tea, museums, and, of course, handkerchiefs. Helen spread out a bevy of her beautiful hankies, and we got lost in the myriad colors and designs.

Helen had an idea for a book—*Hanky Panky*—a chronicle of her personal obsession with handkerchiefs as a reflection of the larger American love affair with the "delicate rag." Her enthusiasm was contagious, and I couldn't wait to see the book.

As the years passed, I often wondered about the fate of *Hanky Panky.* My periodic bookstore investigations turned up two new books by Helen about tea, but there was no sign of her opus on handkerchiefs. Finally in 2000, I contacted Helen for help with an exhibit we were planning in the Marghab Gallery about the history of handkerchiefs—*Handkerchiefs: Mysteries Revealed.* I wanted to talk to someone who shared my excitement about handkerchiefs, but who had a nonacademic angle on how to present historical information to the modern museum visitor.

Shortly after our exhibit opened, Helen wrote to say that *Hanky Panky* was about to be published. Now that I have read the book, I am thrilled to say that it is everything and more than I hoped it would be. I was wise to seek Helen's advice for our exhibit, for what she does so well is blend historical facts and personal memories, thereby creating a fascinating context for both. I am confident you will find *Hanky Panky* unique and inspiring.

And now I'm going to brew myself a pot of tea, find my favorite old handkerchief, and read this lovely book all over again.

Lisa Scholten
Curator of Collections
South Dakota Art Museum

1893 Chicago Exposition, 9½" x 9½", silk.
The stitching was done in front of spectators at the Exposition to demonstrate the precision and fluidity of machine embroidery. The bird is a somewhat fanciful eagle with peacock pretensions. A hanky such as this might have sold for as much as 5 cents!

A child said What is the grass . . .

I guess it is the handkerchief of the Lord,

A scented gift and remembrancer designedly dropped,

Bearing the owner's name someway in the corners, that we may see and remark and say Whose?

—Walt Whitman, from *Song of Myself*

INTRODUCTION

T here were times in the course of writing this book, when I would close my eyes and see hundreds of handkerchiefs floating down out of the sky. Each of these lovely things had a story attached to it, and each story led to another story, and all the stories were connected by gossamer embroidery thread—golden, of course.

I call this an intimate history of the handkerchief because many of the stories herein are quite personal, and because the point of the book is to illuminate the intimate nature of the handkerchief, as both symbol and functional artifact. The handkerchief is much more than a simple piece of clothing. It is virtually an extension of the self.

The sheer beauty of many handkerchiefs makes writing about them superfluous. This volume is, in large part, a celebration of beauty. Women don't collect hundreds of handkerchiefs and scarves because they need them. We love them for their beauty, for how they make us feel, and for what they help us remember. That's why we want lots of them.

I have included all sorts of fascinating historical "facts" and gossip about handkerchiefs, but this book is not intended to be a comprehensive compendium of handkerchief data. For one thing, there's too much of it. For another, it is almost impossible to distinguish fact from rumor. Miniature histories of the handkerchief abound on the Internet and in encyclopedias and are jammed into larger histories of fabrics and fashion. Some of these little summaries focus on Europe and America; some include Persia, China, India, and Japan. The most frustrating thing about them is that they almost never agree with each other.

One "authoritative" historic synopsis claims that an unnamed Venetian lady invented the handkerchief four hundred years ago. She cut a square out of flax and decorated it with lace. But how could she have invented the handkerchief when, according to my trusty *Columbia Encyclopedia* and various other sources, handkerchiefs were in common use in ancient Greece—over two thousand years ago? And what about the frequent references to white handkerchiefs being ceremoniously dropped by Roman dignitaries to start chariot races and other sporting events, while the Roman crowds waved their hankies as visual applause?

Nevertheless, much of the lore is too fascinating not to repeat. For instance, Martha Washington created a promotional handkerchief to help her husband become the first president. In the 1780s, copperplate printing was used on fabric as well as on paper, so Martha had a batch of "George Washington for President" handkerchiefs printed for distribution at the Constitutional Convention of 1787. Shortly after the Founding Fathers got done founding, George was unanimously elected president. He apparently didn't need the handkerchiefs to get the necessary votes, but Martha wasn't taking any chances, or so the story goes. If George is the father of our country, Martha is the mother of political campaign collectibles.

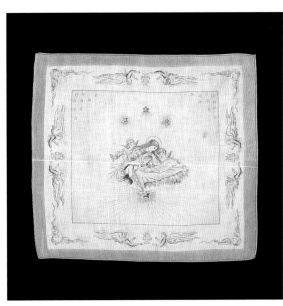

1902, 13¾"x 12½", cotton.
This nativity scene hanky is reminiscent of those given to children as a reward for good behavior. One happy little girl in the 1840s received such a prize for pledging never to use cane sugar processed by slaves.

I wanted to relate the Martha Washington story early on, because most of what I know about handkerchiefs has to do with handkerchiefs in America, and more specifically handkerchiefs in *my* America. I have included personal experiences, family stories (many of them set in the Midwest), and stories told to me by friends and fellow handkerchief fanciers from all over the country. My life, which includes what was told to me by my mother and grandmother and aunties—spans the second half of the nineteenth century, all of the twentieth, and now these first years of the twenty-first! I have been immersed in fashion since I was a little girl, and handkerchiefs have figured importantly all along the way.

The sexual connotations of the expression hanky-panky are ingrained in the American psyche. When I tell people the title of this book, they either

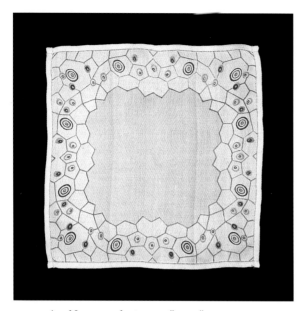

1930s Art Nouveau design, 10" x 10".
Silk dress pocket with exquisitely rendered drawn
work border.

arch their eyebrows or say something like "Ooh la la." But where did the expression come from? As with everything else about handkerchiefs, even the various authorities on the origins of words can't seem to agree about this one. Most concur that hanky-panky came into popular usage in the mid-1800s and was originally synonymous with hocus-pocus, with no sexual implications. However, the highly respected word sleuth Eric Partridge claims that hanky-panky does derive from the word *handkerchief* and refers specifically to magician's sleights of hand employing handkerchiefs. Hocus-pocus, he claims, covers a wider range of conjuring arts. The sexual connotations, some claim, arose in America in the 1940s, but this seems highly unlikely to me. After all, handkerchiefs have been associated with sexual intrigue and intimacy for hundreds, if not thousands, of years.

For instance, there is the tale of Madame de Pompadour and Louis XV, the charismatic king of France from 1710 to 1774. The story goes that Louis was on the prowl for a new mistress, and though the very beautiful Madame Jeanne-Antoinette Poisson was already married, her husband permitted, yet regretted, her making a match with the king. This delicately beautiful lady reputedly gained the king's attention by appearing every day in an open carriage on the edge of the forest, where the king had numerous opportunities to observe her. His interest fired by these continuous sightings, he staged a royal costume ball at which he and several cohorts appeared in identical costumes. They were dressed as trees (as in the trees on the edge of the forest). It was apparently impossible to tell which tree was the king, and various hopeful ladies were grievously disappointed when they discovered that the tree limbs they were nestling in were not the king's. No, Louis had chosen Madame Poisson, who thereafter became known as Madame de Pompadour. The news that he'd made his choice spread quickly through the ballroom on the wings of the expression "the handkerchief has been thrown." By the way, Madame de Pompadour enhanced her tiny face with an upswept, off-the-brow hairstyle, and the pompadour has been so called ever since.

1930s, China, 14½" x 14½", cotton.
The Chinese have a custom of hiding a bird or dragon in their border decorations. I owned this rather quiet hanky for a year before the swan showed herself to me.

This expression, "the handkerchief has been thrown," is one of innumerable instances of the handkerchief representing the bond between lovers. Another dates from medieval times, when the handkerchief worn by a knight competing in a tournament was a symbol of his lady's favor. Guinevere gave Lancelot one of her very best, sweetly scented handkerchiefs to wear when he jousted, and that may have been what tipped off King Arthur to their hanky-panky.

But what is a handkerchief, as opposed to a bandana or a scarf or a napkin? There have never been any hard-and-fast rules defining the exact dimensions of a handkerchief, though another French king, Louis the XVI, did issue a royal decree declaring that all handkerchiefs should be square. No one took him seriously, except maybe his wife Marie Antoinette. She was reportedly the power behind the exclusive decree, and some sources even suggest she invented the lace handkerchief by tearing a piece from a lace curtain in her Austrian home while shedding tears over having to move to France to marry Louis. But the problem with these facts is that they sound so much like gossip, it's often hard to distinguish history from myth.

Most historians do agree that the handkerchief came into general use throughout Europe during the Renaissance (1200–1500) and was no longer just a pretty thing employed by the royal and the rich. Therein is a clue to what a handkerchief is. These Renaissance hankies were originally referred to as *napkyns.* So no matter how elegant or gorgeous or expensive a handkerchief is, it is descended from a long line of functional pieces of cloth, intended for wiping sweaty brows and blowing noses. They were also the so-called *muckminders* of the Elizabethan era (1500s)—used for mopping up baby's messes.In Elizabethan times, Queen Elizabeth's ladies in waiting kept various accoutrements ready for her majesty: scissors, a bodkin, a knife, an ear picker, ropes of pearls, a handkerchief. All these things were attached to a cord that the ladies wore around their waists throughout the day ready for the Queen's use. (In case you don't know what a bodkin is, it's a long blunt pin used to fasten up the hair.)

As to the shape, many handkerchiefs are square, as King Louis XVI decreed they should be, but some are round, others mimic the outlines of flowers, and still others are rectangular. Scarves tend to be longer, if not wider, than most handkerchiefs and are not intended for the absorption of bodily fluids. The line between *bandana* and *handkerchief* is so fine that they are, for the most part, simply different words for the same thing.

Of course, some handkerchiefs are intended only for show, but when push comes to shove—nasal itch turns to sneeze—any hanky is fair game.

For those who grew up before Kleenex tissue completely took over the nasal hygiene scene and

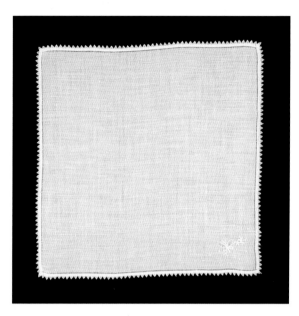

1900, Armenian handmade needle lace, 11" x 10",
cotton. If you lost this hanky in 1902 you might have
said, "Oh well, I have lots more." Lose it today and
you'll tear the house apart to find it.

annihilated the handkerchief industry, this volume
should bring back the glory days of the delicate rag,
when handkerchiefs were an indispensable part of
every woman's wardrobe and toilette. I have yet to
meet a woman over fifty who doesn't have a treasure
trove of handkerchief memories. Most have troves
of handkerchiefs, too.

For those of you born A.K. (after the coming of
Kleenex tissue), consider this: before tattoos, piercings,
and pink and purple and green hair, before tie-dyed
T-shirts, neon leggings, and facial glitter, before all
the hundreds of visible expressions of individuality
now available and acceptable in mainstream society,
the handkerchief was sometimes one of the only ways
to express uniqueness and individuality.

Among all those men in their gray flannel suits
that made the 1950s seem like one big blur, there were those with bright blue or red or green handkerchiefs just peeking over the rims of their pockets. And countless women who dressed within the narrow
confines of acceptable fashion showed their true colors in the flamboyance or subtlety of handkerchiefs
that spoke of their deeper and more passionate natures.

Enter now into the fascinating world of the handkerchief.

1950s, 14½" x 14½", cotton.
Though influenced by Abstract Expressionist art, the design of this piece is not purely abstract. Close scrutiny reveals a forest scene with a path or river snaking through fanciful trees—opening new design possibilities for the traditionally prim "canvas" of the handkerchief.

Handkerchief Boxes

Not to be confused with the wooden boxes made especially for storing handkerchiefs, the boxes used for packaging and displaying hankies were as important to vendors as the handkerchiefs themselves until the 1960s.

HANDKERCHIEFS

1930s, 8¼" x 8¼".
The peachy color of this box came into vogue in the late 1920s. Nightgowns and slips of this color were con
risqué and a cut above cream and white.

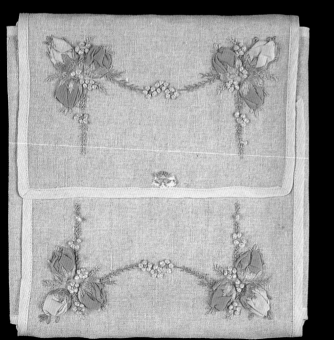

Top left:
1925, 8¼" x 8¼".
Images and silhouettes from the 1800s—hoop skirts and enormous sun bonnets—were widely used on handkerchief boxes and in advertisements for handkerchiefs well into the 20th century.

Top right:
1935, "Ladies' Fine Handkerchiefs," 9¼" x 6¼".
Reminiscent of a candy box suggesting multiple dainties within.

Bottom Left:
1920, linen, 9" x 9".
Ribbon embroidery technique is used to create the roses. Snap closure.

Once upon a time there were three little foxes
Who didn't wear stockings, and they didn't wear sockses,
But they all had handkerchiefs to blow their noses
And they kept their handkerchiefs in cardboard boxes.

—A.A. Milne, from *The Three Foxes*

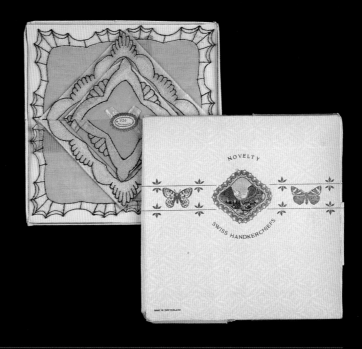

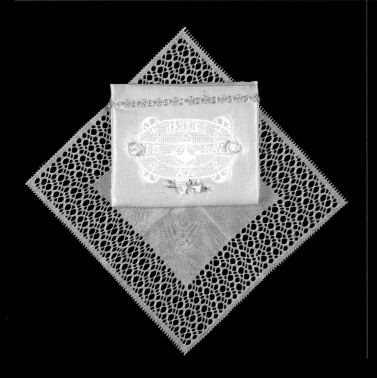

Top right:
1930, 8" x 8".
Swiss manufacturer with "spider web" hanky in box,
as purchased, attached to paper.

Bottom Left:
1980, 11" x 11", polyester.
This hanky and its imitation satin case, in all their
bold yellowanosity, are particularly strident and
insulting. The husband who would buy this for his
wife doesn't even have enough affection for her to
find one that says "to my wife" or "for my wife."
The single word Wife is as perfunctory a label as
Dog or Cat.

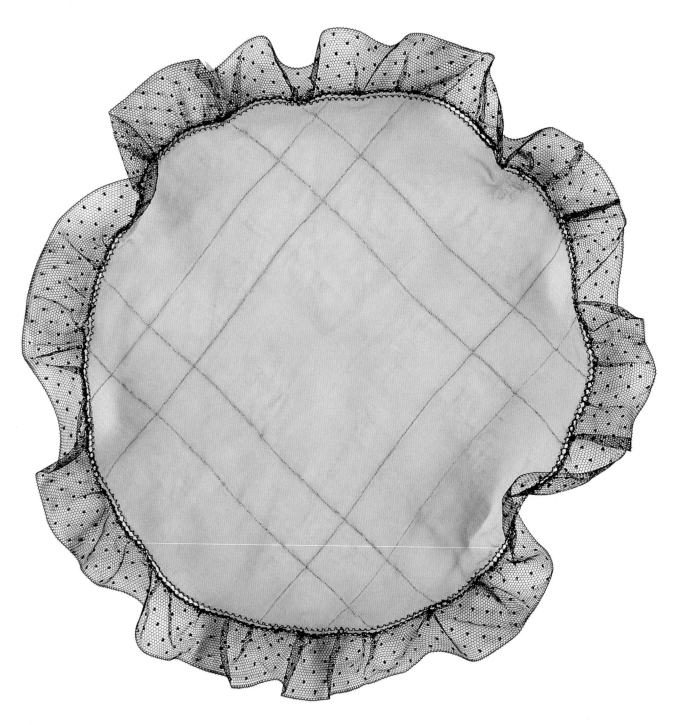

1920, circular 10" diameter handkerchief of cotton lawn, embellished with drawn work and trimmed with black point d'espirit net. From the collection of the Oakland Museum of California.

A Micro History

(Representing a collection of the author's favorite historic tidbits about the handkerchief, some of which may even be true.)

OF THE HANDKERCHIEF

• 1000 B.C. The emperor and the upper class of the Chinese Chou dynasty use rectangular pieces of cloth decorated with fringes.

• 50 B.C. Handkerchiefs are used commonly by Roman men. It would be another hundred years or so before Roman women, at the height of the empire, also carry hand-kerchiefs for everyday use.

That handkerchief
Did an Egyptian to my mother give.
—William Shakespeare, from *Othello*

• 700 B.C. The Persian hand-kerchief is a sign of royalty and is the exclusive domain of the king and nobility.

• Having eaten of the forbidden fruit, Adam and Eve use fig leaves to cover their shame. Could these have been the first hankies?

• 100 B.C. Handkerchiefs are used by the highest class in Greece as a fashionable luxury. These squares of cloth are probably decorated in some way to distinguish them from the rags used by the lower classes.

• 300–500 The decline and fall of the Roman Empire accompany the decline and fall of the use of handkerchiefs.

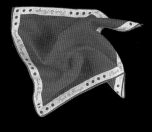

• 1000 The handkerchief becomes a gift of betrothal similar to the modern engagement ring.

• 1400 The Renaissance brings about a resurgence of the handkerchief throughout Europe—used by both sexes within a wide range of social classes.

• 33 A.D. As depicted in the paintings of the Sixth Station of the Cross, Veronica the Compassionate presents Jesus with a handkerchief to wipe away his blood and sweat.

• 1100–1300 In the late Middle Ages, the handkerchief is a prized possession, ostentatiously displayed by the wealthy.

• 500–900 During the Dark Ages, handkerchiefs give way to the shirtsleeve for wiping sweat and other bodily fluids. Monks, nuns, and the few remaining people possessed of social graces still enjoy the use of handkerchiefs.

• 1500 Handkerchiefs figure prominently in all royal courts in the world.

• 1679 Milan Council decrees that Venetian needlepoint should be used only for handkerchiefs. This is one of many attempts by the rich and powerful to keep the handkerchief an exclusive possession of the wealthy, and to distinguish it from the more common hand cloths used by common folk. To no avail.

• 1600s Lace borders are the most common means of distinguishing handkerchiefs of the wealthy from those of the poor.

• 1785 Invention of the roller printer revolutionizes the handkerchief world. Hankies are now printed with pictures, slogans, logos, maps, flags, and virtually anything can be printed on paper.

• 1570 Disgusted by the continued use of the sleeve for sweat and nose wiping, Queen Elizabeth I orders that the sleeves of all soldiers' uniforms have big buttons sewed every few inches along the arms to discourage the use of the sleeve for purposes better suited to handkerchiefs.

• 1604 Shakespeare writes his tragedy *Othello*, in which Desdemona and her handkerchief figure prominently.

• 1780 Louis XVI decrees all handkerchiefs should be square. No one listens to him.

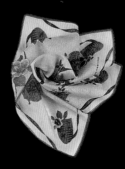

• 1700s The international snuff craze coincides with the Industrial Revolution, creating a massive market for factory-made handkerchiefs.

1910, Puerto Rico, 9½" x 9½", cotton.
A child's handkerchief with a most telling price tag. Nearly all the handkerchiefs "Made in America" between 1900 and 1940 were actually crafted in Puerto Rico by women being paid unimaginably low wages, per piece, by New York manufacturers. The meticulous appliqué work and hand stitching could not have been done hastily.

• 1973 Monty Python produces the album *Matching Tie and Handkerchief,* with which they give away a matching tie and handkerchief.

• 2000 Having survived the last thirty years as a kind of cult relic and still employed by sensible people over the age of fifty, the handkerchief emerges once again as an indispensable accessory for savvy folks navigating the wild times of the new millennium.

• 1800–1955 The Golden Age of Handkerchiefs. Everyone everywhere has them.

• 1965–75 Hippies employ paisley handkerchiefs to tie up their long hair and for use as headbands. People with a sense of classic style continue to carry handkerchiefs and value them as fashion accessories. Those without class or taste switch to wasteful boxes of tissue paper.

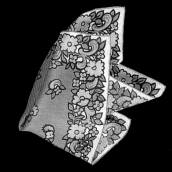

• 1956–65 The growing popularity of Kleenex does not immediately undermine the use of the handkerchief for those who grew up with them and loved them, but the writing is on the wall, or on the tissue paper.

1970s, 14" x 14", cotton.
The cartoon style of rendering leaves and flowers, and this particular combination of colors, spring from the neo-deco pop art popularized by artists creating posters for folk rock concerts in the late 1960s and early 1970s. Hand-rolled edge, with a tag that reads *The Emporium, $1.00.*

$\mathscr{I}$ $\mathscr{K}$NEW
I HAD IT BAD

$\mathscr{A}$t a garage sale in the early 1980s, when I was in my fifties, I impulsively bought this small, ragged handkerchief with the outline of the flower forming its border. These flower-shaped handkerchiefs were wildly popular in the late 1930s and '40s. The thing was in tatters, but I had to have it. That "had to have it" feeling was proof I'd been bitten once again by the collector's bug. All those amorous reds and pinks enticed and intrigued me

So there I was, sitting on the front stoop of our farm in South Dakota, literally piecing that old handkerchief together, when Wilma, my closest neighbor—a mile and three-quarters away— walked up and with no preamble asked, "What are you doing?"

I answered, "I'm mending this handkerchief." She allowed that I was doing just that, we chatted for a bit, and then she went away.

A few days later, she turned up with a gift for me: a brand-new, heavily laced, machine-made hand-kerchief from the dime store, on which she had crocheted a pretty border. She nodded sympathetically and said, "I had no idea things were so hard for you."

This ragged piece was the first of my Big Flower collection. Once, showing off a stack of these handkerchiefs to two enthusiasts, we had to stop and catch our breaths after ten minutes. All that oohing and aahing had brought on hyperventilation.

1940, 11" x 10", cotton, mended by author.

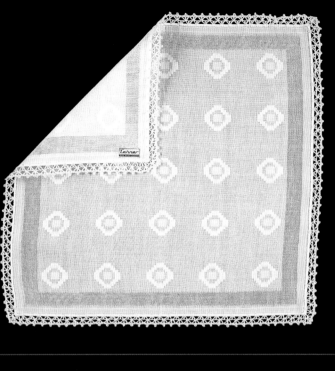

Top left:
1980, Switzerland, 13" x 13", cotton.
Purchased in a variety store in South Dakota,
my neighbor Wilma embellished this simple piece
with coordinated crochet work to make it special.

Top right:
1930s, 9½" x 10".
Authentic homemade hanky. Cotton sheeting is
embellished with a crocheted border.

Bottom right:
Embroidery and woven label detail.

1940s, 12" x 12", cotton, machine hemmed.
Open weave technique creates a textural effect.

My First Handkerchief

Sevilla, my father's mother—noble, kind, large boned, and handsome—gave me the first handkerchief I could call my very own. I was ten. Everything about the gift and the way it was presented to me was in keeping with her splendid character and her challenging life experiences. I knew without question that her misspelling of my name—Hellen—had nothing to do with her intelligence, which was formidable, but rather her lack of formal education. I kept my mouth shut about the extra "L".

She had lived through three great economic depressions and had developed the art of wasting nothing to an awesome degree. After she died, her daughters found in a kitchen drawer a little envelope labeled "Pieces of string too short to save." Pitiful but amusing.

The handkerchief she gave me, a simple cotton one in blue and white—the colors of sincerity—came in the mail as a surprise. No tissue paper, no ribbon, no note. Just my name on a scrap of paper affixed with a pin to a left-over piece of apron edging.

Yet I was enraptured by the gift. I made me feel dignified, just like the hanky. And it brought back memories of Sevilla, on visits to the farm, who would often take me by the hand and softly stroke my arm, looking at me as if I were an angel descended from heaven, and sweetly call me "Girlie" as we made plans to gather eggs or make ice cream. Is it any wonder I thought of her as a family saint?

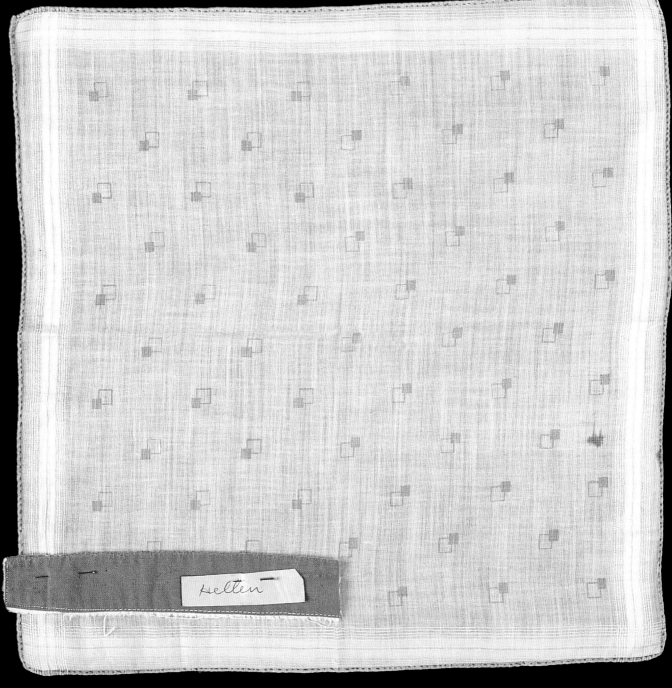

1930, 11" x 11", cotton.
Purchased in the dime store for no more than five cents, this gift was typical of my grandmother Sevilla. "Nothing too fancy." Note the hand rolled hem.

SNUFF

Taking (snorting) snuff (tobacco) became all the rage in England in the 1700s. The widespread use of this highly addictive substance and the sneezy mess it created presented the British textile industry with a great opportunity—a vastly expanded market for handkerchiefs. Before the snuff era, women's handkerchiefs were intended exclusively for special occasions and were traditionally little lacy white squares. But with the coming of snuff, a larger square of fabric—often cotton from India—was required, and the handkerchief became a major fashion accessory for both men and women.

Because snuff stains were visible against a white background, colored handkerchiefs came into vogue. Rich golden browns, maroons, and intense yellows were very popular. Although snuff would pass out of public favor a few generations later—a link to nasal cancer was established—by then the handkerchief had become a fashion cornerstone and would reign supreme until the growing popularity of Kleenex in the 1950s.

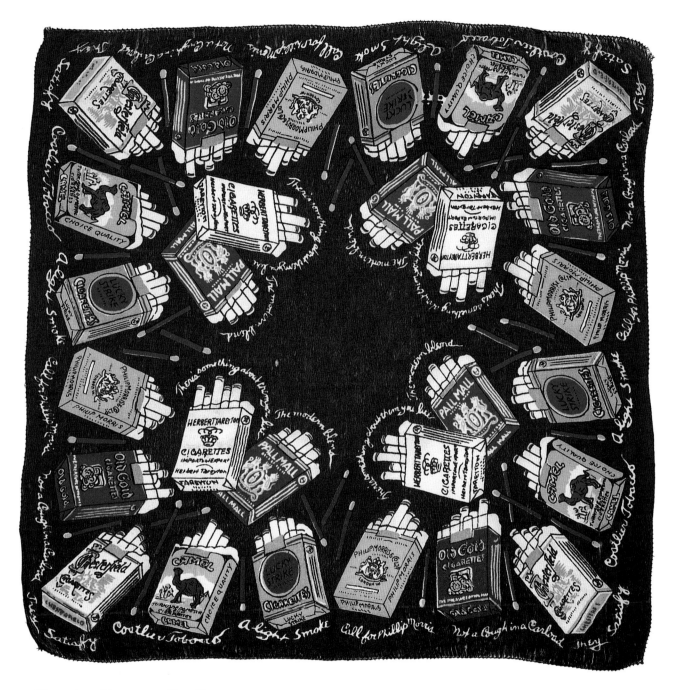

Unusual crinkle cotton, 16" x 16"

The green Lucky Strike pack marks this as pre-1940. The green dye was more urgently needed for the war effort.

To publicize the change Lucky Strike launched a white pack with the slogan *Lucky Strike Green has gone to war!* Some of the more amusing slogans on this piece include: *Eat a chocolate, light a cigarette, and enjoy both! Two fine and healthful treats;* and *Not a Cough in a Carload.* From the collection of Winifred and Phil Wood.

Morning and Mourning

There's a difference.

Had you been a lady getting ready for your morning ride or walk in the 1800s, you would have been careful to select your handkerchief from the "everyday" collection. This assortment would have included white lawn and even humble muslin pieces with rolled hems. Some might have been decorated with plain bobbin lace from Belgium, or the borders might have been painted with a few colored flowers to coordinate with the colors of your outfit. Heaven forbid that you should be seen sporting a more elegant handkerchief for a casual outing. Such a lapse would have been considered vulgar, even scandalous, and might have resulted in unfriendly gossip and negative social repercussions.

Mourning handkerchiefs are bordered with black edges or black ribbons, for obvious reasons.

Where a blood relation sobs, an intimate friend should choke up, a distant acquaintance should sigh, a stranger should merely fumble sympathetically with his handkerchief.

—Mark Twain, on etiquette at a funeral.

1940s, 12" x 11¾", cotton.
This piece is a hybrid of the stark, black-edged hankies popular in the early part of the 20th century, and the simple white ones used at funerals today. It appears that the designer couldn't resist taking a lighter stance by adding graceful white flourishes.

Over There

My great-aunts Vida, Vera, and Sevilla, all small-town beauties, each had sweethearts "over there" —fighting in Europe during World War I. The sisters were born in the early 1900s when Washington Irving's *Tales of the Alhambra* was phenomenally popular, hence, the preponderance of Spanish names. Bianca was a popular name, too, mangled in the local Nebraska vernacular as By-ant-sa. The world there was rather narrow in scope. I remember one aunt saying, "Now Margarita is very nice—she *is* a Catholic— but she's very nice."

Vida was the first to receive a handkerchief, a typical gift, from her "fellow" (not boyfriend, not fiancé). It was a gossamer silk piece in a lovely somber gray. Eventually Vera and Sevilla received handkerchiefs, too, though not as big and fine as Vida's.

Vida never married, her beloved having died in the war. She lived with her sister Sevilla for the rest of her days in a house built especially for them.

Forty years after World War I ended, Vida was cleaning out a drawer full of old things when she found the *Remember Me* handkerchief in a little box, untouched since the news of her sweetheart's death. This fragile keepsake fell apart into many little squares as she lifted it from the box, the delicate silk breaking along the lines where it had been creased.

As the pieces fluttered to the floor, Vida began to weep. Sevilla, always nearby, poked her head into the room to give Vida a long, questioning look. Vida would only say she'd gotten a bit of dust in her eyes and continued her sorting.

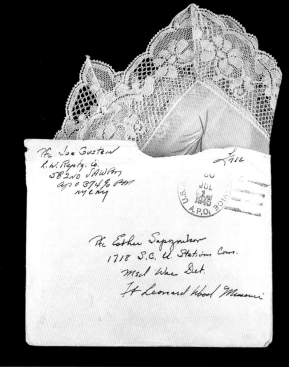

Top left & right:
1945, Belgium, 10" x 11", silk.
"To my dear wife!" This marvelous piece was sent
from Belgium to America at the end of World War II
by an American soldier who made it home alive. The
lavish lace border and the tiny sparkly Bedazzlers at
the centers of the flowers, as well as the hand painting
of the words and date, place this among the most lavish
of the wartime souvenirs and bespeak a true love.

Bottom left:
1917, England, 14½" x 14 ½".
Made of inexpensive silk, these touching "picturettes"
were not ever intended to be used, but rather shown
off in a purse or pocket, or framed and displayed on
a dresser top.

$\mathcal{L}$ILY $\mathcal{P}$ONS

In the 1950s, I lived in a very romantic, artistic, third-floor studio apartment in a Manhattan brownstone. I was studying voice, and my teacher lived downstairs. When she invited me to peruse the contents of a trunk she'd inherited from the Metropolitan Opera—costumes and accoutrements originally used by Lily Pons—my eyes opened wide. What a find! Delicate little Lily Pons, the belle of the opera world during my childhood. We looked at the costumes; armpits brown with dried perspiration, dresses stained with food, but all very beautiful. I remember an elegant collar, ragged and torn, on a lace dressing gown with woven and twisted ribbon roses rising a good half inch above the collar.

At the bottom of the box was a crumpled-up handkerchief, deeply stained with makeup. It had rose color on it and skin color on it, and it was scented with the heavy-grease paint odor common to all theatrical makeup of that time. I smelled the handkerchief, and suddenly the opera came rushing into me: the noise of the taxis, the shouting of stage attendants, the bright lights, the sweat, the hubbub of life in the theater—all swirling around this crumpled mass of delicate cotton.

I never washed it. I never ironed it. I just tucked it away. I still get it out now and then to let all that drama come back to me.

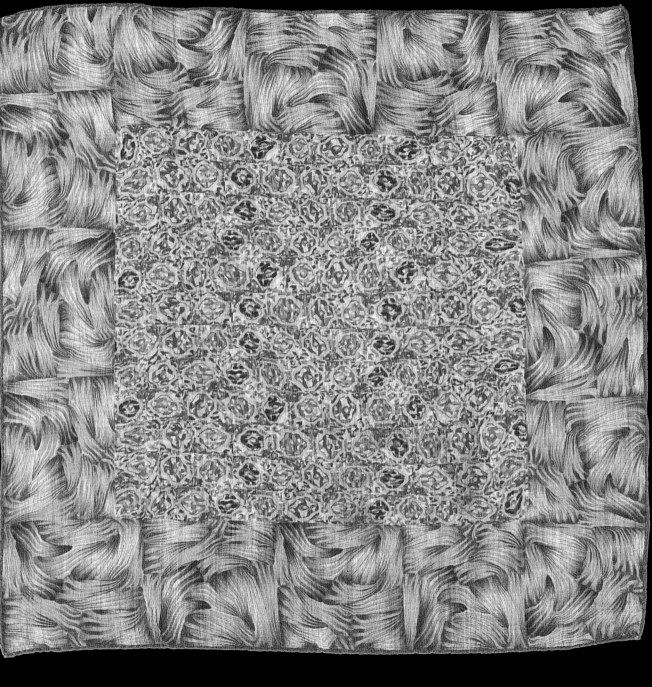

Cotton multi-color print, 12" x 13".
Probably silk-screened, the unusual design creates the illusion of one handkerchief atop another. Although hard to date, this hanky is possibly from the 1950s, when Miss Pons was at her peak.

1918, 16½" x 17", airplane linen with simple drawn work.
Made by the author's mother.

AIRPLANE LINEN

When I was a girl in the 1940s, my mother would occasionally take me on an exciting jaunt to the warehouse district of downtown Saint Paul, to the exotic old army-navy surplus store. Far from chic, it was actually a scary dungeon of piled-up junk.

Mother once bought what looked like a small stack of pale wooden planks. They were actually heavy, natural linen, untreated, made to last forever, and they were very inexpensive. The linen was used mainly to cover World War I airplane wings. At home, after hundreds of washings, this incredibly sturdy material became paler and paler and softer and softer. But in the beginning, it was literally as stiff as a board.

During the Great Depression, everything that came one's way and could be put to use was. Those surplus linens, once softened, were turned into tablecloths, linings of jackets and hats, inner pillow protectors, curtains, and pajamas. I inherited a dozen airplane linen napkins. Clever woman, my mother, she made them of an intermediate size so that when they were very old, they could be used as handkerchiefs. Sometimes an oblong place mat (if not too stained) was cut in half to make two handkerchiefs.

When I first used these napkins in the 1950s, I was slightly embarrassed to think that my guests might recognize them as reminders of those harder times. Now, these old linens make quaint conversation pieces and a look into the past when

Use it up

Wear it out

Make it do

Or do without

. . . was a bit of everyday wisdom.

SHOW AND BLOW

Beginning in the late 1800s in rural America and continuing well into the 1900s, children were required to bring clean handkerchiefs to school. Because it was no easy matter to always have a clean handkerchief on hand, mothers hit upon the idea of sending their children to school with two handkerchiefs—a clean one to show the teacher and a working handkerchief that could stand up to frequent washings.

These hankies became known as Blow and Show, though some folks recall them as Show and Blow. The last words children heard as they left the house for school were, "Do you have your show and blow?"

One friend remembers that she kept her white show hanky (a rag really, but neatly folded to conceal the holes) clipped inside the top of her lunch box. By the end of the school year it was so gray and stinky she just threw it away. Her blow handkerchief—a cheerful blue and white check good at disguising stains—was laundered once a week and just got softer and sweeter over time.

As it happens, a similar show-and-blow practice exists in Japan. In classical Japanese dress, a little pocket inside the left sleeve of the lady's kimono is for keeping a functional handkerchief, usually white. The pocket in her right sleeve holds a beautiful colored handkerchief for display only. In addition, a gorgeous color coordinated square of fabric is often tucked into the middle V opening at the neck for a color accent.

The handkerchief has never gone out of vogue in Japan, and the displays of handkerchiefs in enormous department stores are breathtaking walls of beauty.

Oh, yes, the handle of the knife used for committing hara-kiri (ritual suicide) in Japan is traditionally sheathed in a pure white handkerchief.

Left: 1920, 11" x 12", cotton. Typical gingham check, machine hemmed.
Right: 1950, 15 ⅛" x 16 ⅛", cotton, machine hemmed.

Gold Miner

It was a gray-sky blustery day not long ago, rather an English sort of day, as I was walking to the local library to look up the history of the classic curvy design known as paisley. So many bandanas, handkerchiefs, shawls, cravats, ties, and blouses are fashioned with this design; I wanted to know more.

As I crossed the street, I suddenly saw a handkerchief tumbling along the street, pushed toward me by a cold breeze. Then the pretty little thing stopped right at my feet! I snatched it up and gasped in amazement. The color and the imprinted spangles marked it as modern, but the classic paisley print might have been a thousand years old.

I didn't make it to the library but went directly home to wash the handkerchief. As I studied my find, I noted the crease in the fabric where it had been folded to make a headband showing off the spangles. I imagined that this inexpensive piece had recently adorned some cute brunette who wore it to match her pink turtleneck and pendulous purple earrings.

The term *paisley* refers to the town of Paisley, Scotland, where paisley shawls were produced in enormous quantities throughout the 1800s, when shawls, especially those featuring this ancient design, were fashionable throughout Europe. The paisley pattern originated in Kashmir (a province of ancient Persia, now northern India), where shawls of this kind have been woven since the eleventh century. The motif can be found in Kashmiri rugs from even earlier times.

The design of this contemporary paisley handkerchief has been around for at least a couple hundred years. This particular piece is not the dark blue worn by California gold miners in the 1800s, and it is not the cheerful green of the Girl Scout handkerchiefs so common in the 1950s and '60s. Nor is it the barn red kerchief worn around the necks of cowboys. No, this lavender is a thoroughly modern color, and the little spangles called Bedazzlers have been impressed with some new technology that ensures they will never come off, no matter how many times they are assaulted by the washing machine.

Top left:
1980s, 19¾" x 20¼", cotton.
Paisley design with adhered Bedazzlers.

Top right:
1940, 12" x 13", cotton. The bucking bronco is a dominant cowboy symbol. These eye-catching hand-kerchiefs and bandanas are commonly sold at rodeos and in Western wear shops. From the collection of Heather Hafleigh.

Bottom left:
1990, 21½" x 21½", cotton.
Symbols of the West—bucking broncos, cactus, sagebrush, cowboy hats—repeat at the four corners surrounding a central motif to create a mandala effect that pulls the eye to the center. From the collection of Heather Hafleigh.

1932, 11" x 10", white organdy.
Details made from one hanky cut into four pieces and machine-finished.

WEDDING APRONS

It was during the hot, desperate summer of 1932 in a barren little town in Nebraska—the day before The Wedding—when this charming apron was made. This scenario of a last-minute wedding was common, acted out again and again across the Great Plains.

There is a pause at the end of the growing season, just before the actual harvest, when everything stops and waits. It was during this dead time that my aunt reluctantly but bravely agreed with the family's suggestion that since Grandma was having a good spell and Cousin Della May was on hand to help, they should have the wedding then and there, at home.

The subtext of saving money on a church wedding with store-bought flowers and a wedding dress was never mentioned. But the potential for trouble poisoned the already tense atmosphere. Would Grandma stay well? What about the weather and the dust storms? And who would come?

My aunt quickly chose four bridesmaids from among friends and cousins. Translation: she asked four waitresses not only to stand up with her but also to bustle about serving coffee, lemonade, cookies, and cake. Matching dresses for the bridesmaids were out of the question, so according to the latest fashion, each made her own apron in sheer white organdy. At least the apron pattern was fashionable. There was no time to embroider flowers on the aprons, but

1900–2002, lady-in-a-cape doll, 7" x 6".
This doll may have a small wooden or cotton insert to give form to the head, but many hanky dolls were made from a simple handkerchief folded into a doll form on the spot in church to occupy a restless child.

Cousin Della May, who was well-off, produced four pretty hankies from Paris, France (not Paris, Ohio), which she'd picked up on her honeymoon. Each was cut into four pieces, supplying the pocket and trim.

One almost wicked secret in all the goings-on was that the bride persuaded her sister to go to "town," Omaha, the day before the wedding to purchase a picture hat. It would be white, of course, a lacy wide-brimmed affair just like the one Myrna Loy wore in the movies. It was my aunt's only frivolous expense.

They spent the whole stifling day walking the broiling pavement in their best clothes, their feet in high-heeled agony, looking for the perfect hat.

At the end of the day, they triumphantly found it—and for this one time, never mind the price—and headed for the train and home, exultant.

Everyone was up at five A.M. for the baking and the cleaning, and miraculously everything was finished just in time. The ceremony came off without a hitch—no tornado, no dust storm, Grandma lasted, everybody came, the house was packed, and the cookies held out.

It was after the wedding that the sisters found the four aprons neatly laid out on the bed in the spare room, with the picture hat set at a jaunty angle on the bedpost. All had been forgotten.

Later, the aprons were a big help at a funeral and one wedding, but the hat was never worn, and the bride could never speak of it again.

One of the aprons was handed down to me. Note the precise machine stitching of the quartered handkerchief. By then, skill with a sewing machine had become as valued as ordinary handwork.

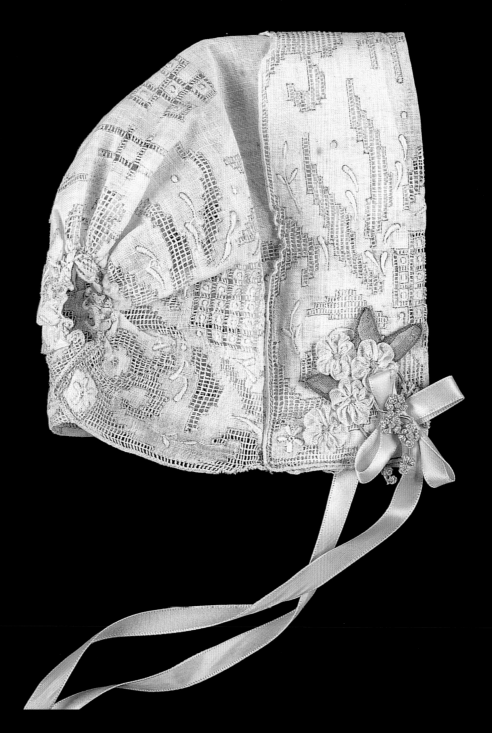

1980, baby bonnet, made from a Chinese cotton handkerchief.
Note the ambiguous trim making it acceptable for a girl or a boy. From the collection of Chandra Cho.

Sign Language

By the late 1890s, handkerchiefs were so well established that they were used for all sorts of non-verbal communications. A list of interpretations, circa 1905, ran as follows:

Drawing across the lips—*I desire to make your acquaintance.*

Drawing across the eyes—*I am sorry.*

Dropping—*We will be friends.*

Twirling in both hands—*Indifference.*

Drawing across cheek—*I love you.*

Drawing through hand—*I hate you.*

Resting on right cheek—*Yes.*

Resting on left cheek—*No.*

Twisting in left hand—*I wish to get rid of you.*

Twisting in right hand—*I love another.*

Folding—*I wish to speak with you.*

Over the shoulder—*Follow me.*

Opposite corners in both hands—*Wait for me.*

Drawing across forehead—*We are watched.*

Placing on right ear—*You have changed.*

Letting it remain on the eyes—*You are cruel.*

Winding around forefinger—*I am engaged.*

Winding around third finger—*I am married.*

Putting in the pocket—*No more at present.*

The potential for comical or disastrous misinterpretations and mistakes was enormous. But if you find this silent vocabulary farfetched, remember that a hundred years ago, open communication between the sexes was a revolutionary idea.

Fast forward to the late twentieth century when millions of gays and lesbians in America and Europe came out of their closets to openly celebrate their sexual preferences. By the mid-1970s a much more risqué form of handkerchief sign language was being used in the gay party and club scene. For example a handkerchief dangling from the right pants pocket (hip or front) meant that the dangler preferred to be submissive. If the hanky dangled from the left pocket, the dangler preferred to be dominant.

1950, four-heart Valentine, 19" diameter, cotton.
Hankies were a favorite gift item all year round, but on Valentine's day they were a popular and potent symbol for love.

QUEEN VICTORIA'S MORALS

*H*istoric rumor has it that Queen Victoria, circa 1868, was riding in her carriage at a military review, accompanied by her daughter, the Princess Royal, a headstrong girl of thirteen. The princess, sitting on the front seat of the carriage, began to flirt openly with some of the younger officers of their mounted escort. The queen made disapproving faces at her daughter, but these didn't repress the princess.

Finally, the princess resorted to the classic flirtation of dropping her handkerchief over the side of the carriage, causing three gallant officers to leap from their horses to rescue the dainty piece of lace.

"Stop!" said the queen, raising an imperious hand to the sky. "Leave it where it lies. Now Daughter, get down from the carriage and reclaim your handkerchief."

Despite her daughter's protests that such an action was beneath her station, Victoria would not relent, and the princess, deeply embarrassed, descended to the ground and retrieved her handkerchief.

Myth or history? In either case, the tale solidifies Queen Victoria's reputation for being an impeccably moral ruler and mother, guided by a firm belief that delinquent tendencies must be nipped in the bud.

1950s, 10¼" x 10", cotton.
The super-abundance of machine open weave imparts a transparency and sense of refinement to this humble flower design and machine-stitched hem.

GEISHAS

Once upon a time, at a prestigious museum, I thrilled to the touch of a natural silk handkerchief with delicate embroidery along the edges. In one of its corners, the fabric appeared to be torn, and the damage covered by a loose flap of silk. Upon closer examination, I saw that the flap was a silk butterfly poised over a neatly finished round hole. The curator, speaking about this remarkable design as if it were commonplace, explained that gesturing with the handkerchief caused a rush of air to flow through the hole and make the butterfly flutter.

Can you see it—the lovely geisha sitting with a client at a corner table in a teahouse, feigning innocence, her eyes cast down, while the butterfly on her handkerchief seductively flutters up?

Handkerchiefs employing this fluttering butterfly, or those with butterfly designs in one corner, have become common in the world of handkerchiefs, though it is not widely known that the design originated with the geishas.

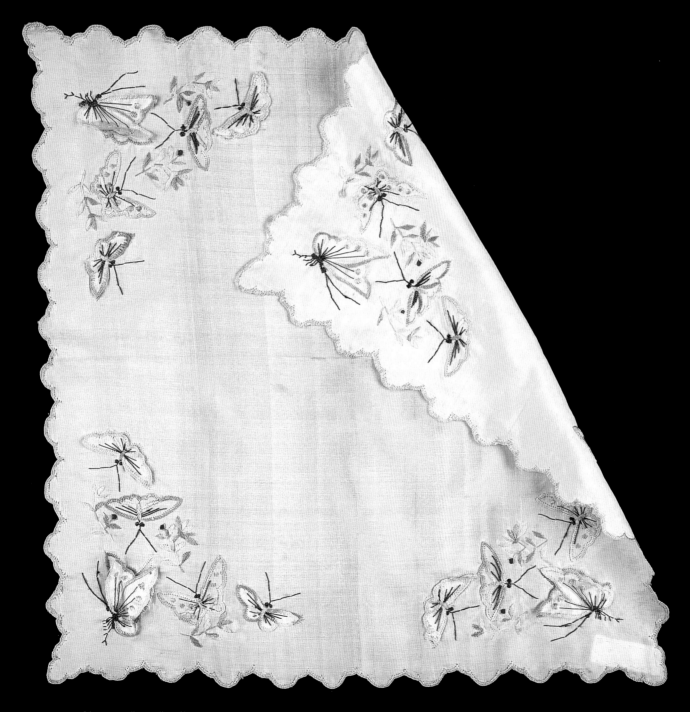

1910, China, 12" x 12", silk.
Plain weave ivory colored silk with cotton pearl twist embroidery; the butterflies have separate appliquéd wings. From
the collection of the Oakland Museum of California.

1990s, Japanese modern, 16" x 16", cotton.
Junko Koshino is one of Japan's leading female fashion designers in an industry dominated by men. Widely admired for her combinations of geometric forms and forms occurring in nature. Her core colors are red and black, and she is most interested in imbuing functional artifacts with a spiritual essence.

Japanese modern, 16" x 16½", cotton.
Yukiko Hanai is another of the prominent women designers in Japan today. Her favorite color is black, and many of her designs are in black and white. She is known for her expressive, spontaneous style.

Kenzie design, Japanese modern, 16" x 16", cotton.

1990, 15½" x 16", fine linen.
A modern variant on the geisha butterfly design. Note the impressed lines on the butterfly replacing more expensive hand embroidery.

1985, Japan, 11" x 10½", cotton.
An amazing piece in that it is not so much embroidered as it is embroidery.

Sonya's Sad Triumph

The mail-order bride stepped off the train from New York onto a narrow wooden platform, and looked about at the mud and the rutted roads—as desolate and cold as Siberia. It was actually Hibbing, Minnesota, in the late 1800s, in the Iron Range Country. When referring to Hibbing, folks in Saint Paul and Minneapolis always did so with a doleful lifting of the head, a sigh, and then, "yah, up there on the range," followed by silence and a nod. Everybody knew how awful it was.

The bride, whose name was Sonya, cried for three weeks and then quietly married the Polish fellow who had sent for her—a sweet, even-tempered owner of a dry goods store. Sonya was from Poland, too, and a professional embroideress. Despite her sorrow at feeling so displaced, she began to produce a family, as well as modest but perfectly finished embroidered pieces: handkerchiefs were her specialty.

Seen among a collection of traditional white, these cream colored handkerchiefs and Sonya's

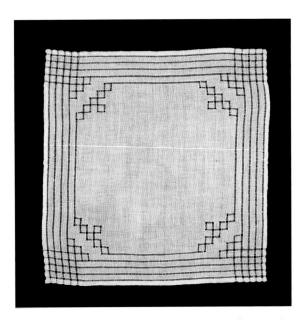

1920s, 11" x 10½", linen. Hand-stitched drawn work.

distinctive embroidery style stand out, even to the untrained eye. Notice how soft, open, and loopy her drawn work is. There are none of the hard edges you will find in most Swiss or Belgian drawn work.

During Sonya's long life in Hibbing, every newly married couple received from her a gift of a twelve-place tablecloth with monogrammed napkins to match, and every new baby, a sweetly embroidered little bonnet. Her gifts and her marvelous character endeared her to everyone in town.

There's a prequel to Sonya's story too delicious not to include. It begins in Poland some years before her arrival in Hibbing. Three brothers, fleeing the invading Russian forces, set out for the New World in a horse-drawn carriage. Two days into their journey, they discovered they were headed for China, not France! Because it seemed too dangerous to turn back, they continued eastward. The journey to America would take three years. One brother stayed in Russia and married there. Another found Japan irresistible and settled there with a Japanese wife. Brother number three, our hero, soldiered on to San Francisco to join the gold rush but arrived thirty years too late. Momentarily disappointed, he perked up when someone described the boom times in the "new" iron mines in Minnesota. He raced across the country, only to arrive in Hibbing twenty years after the boom.

He settled there anyway, saw the need for a dry goods store, and went into business, beginning by sending away for his Polish bride. He was a big success. His second son, Arthur Ballet, was my professor of Theatre Arts at the University of Minnesota. He later became the director of the theatre program of the National Endowment for the Arts. Voila.

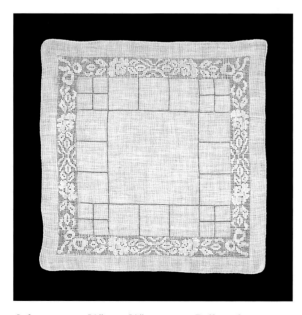 

Left: 1920s, 10¾" x 10¾" , cotton. Pull work.
Right: 1930s, 11¾" x 10¾" , cotton. This example of Muttie's crochet work, so full of her vigorous life force, contrasts sharply with the sad softness of Sonya's work.

WHITES

One could write a whole book just about white handkerchiefs. And though I enjoy looking at the unique and sometimes astonishing ways in which white handkerchiefs are decorated, I'm much more susceptible to beautiful combinations of colors. I say this to explain the scarcity of white handkerchiefs in this book. They are ever so slightly boring to me. I'll take a voluptuous Georgia O'Keeffe iris over an empty canvas any day. I've always preferred fields of wildflowers to orderly displays of white tulips. So here are some lovely whites to know about.

A plain white handkerchief is the sure sign of a confident and elegant dresser.
—Alan Fusser, On return of breast-pocket handkerchiefs in men's suit coats, *International Herald Tribune*, December 31, 1978

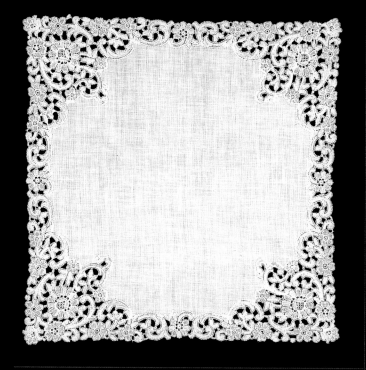

Top left:
1940s, Belgium, 11" x 11", linen.
Rose point bobbin lace, machine lace imitation.

Top right:
1940s, Portugal, 12" x 12", cotton.
Appliqué with interior shadow appliqué.

Bottom left:
1920s French lace and netting, 10" x 10",
machine embroidered net.
This piece was Sevilla's second gift to me.

1990. American import, 17" x 16", polyester/cotton.

Gustafson HANKY PANKY

ITZHAK PERLMAN'S HANDKERCHIEF

It was a memorable event. Itzhak Perlman was in the Flatbush area of Brooklyn giving a free concert on the street in the ersatz village square. Everybody was there: Orthodox Jews, Hasidic Jews, passersby—the whole neighborhood. Perlman emerged from his car like a bear from his cave, looked around in some confusion until he found the chair set out for him, opened his violin case, and took out his priceless instrument. Suddenly he stopped, dumbfounded, and muttered, "My white handkerchief. I can't play without it." He pointed to his chin. "I need one. A clean one!"

Everyone understood, but helplessness prevailed. Wide-eyed looks were exchanged, and the crowd began to stir restlessly. Then from back in the crowd, a young bearded man pushed his way forward, his face tense and drawn, a neatly folded white handkerchief in his hand. "My uncle," he said, jerking his thumb back at where he'd come from. "I knew he'd have one."

Everyone turned to catch a glimpse of this miracle man, so old-fashioned, so elegant—the savior. The moment Perlman got the handkerchief, he began to play, and the uncle was forgotten in a rush of vibrant, vivacious sounds of Klezmer tunes.

What was the fate of that handkerchief? Did our hero get it back? Was he too shy to approach the famous Perlman? Was this brief moment the high point of his life, a story he would embroider into an epic over time? I wish I knew.

J.P. Morgan Waltz

In the early 1900s, when J. P. Morgan and his ilk delighted in inventing new rules for dress—and the refrain "Never wear diamonds with beige in the daytime" was, among the wealthy, not satire. The rules were strict, and the very large, soft, perfectly plain handkerchief had a specific function.

At fancy dress balls, a true gentleman would bring out a spacious, white lawn handkerchief embroidered with his initials. He would fold it into a four-inch square and interpose it between his hand—which might be sweaty—and the bottom edge of the back of his partner's gown. Some gentlemen wore white gloves for the same purpose.

At the end of the waltz, she would open her reticule—a small beaded bag suspended from her pinkie finger by two slender drawstrings—and bring forth a delicate hankie of her own with which she would dab under her chin or at the sides of her nose. Any real mopping up in public was unthinkable.

1890s, 21" x 21", cotton lawn.
Diamond Jim Brady was a famous turn-of-the-century boulevardier (man about town) who frequented the most elite New York social circles. He was It! Handsome, dashing, and a fantastic dresser. No social event of those times could be considered a success without an appearance by Diamond Jim.

The Jewish Wedding

In many of Isaac Bashevis Singer's stories about Jewish life in Poland before the Holocaust, the handkerchief plays a vital role. His father was a rabbi who conducted religious ceremonies in the family's tiny apartment in Warsaw, so the young Isaac was witness to many of the intricacies of Jewish tradition.

The wedding contract is covered with a handkerchief, and the groom signifies his taking responsibility for his bride-to-be by removing the handkerchief. Once the contract is signed, the wedding ceremony can take place.

This ceremony, performed beneath a simple canopy, ends with the groom stepping out from under the canopy and stomping on a wineglass rolled up in a handkerchief. There are many theories for this ritual, the two most popular are to commemorate the temple's destruction and to suggest a reminder of life's fragility.

The wedding dance begins with the newlyweds holding opposite ends of a large handkerchief and gazing at each other as they dance, the handkerchief signifying the new bond between them.

If later in life the couple wishes to divorce, they come before the rabbi to state their complaints, each touching the rabbi's handkerchief to signify that they will agree with his judgment of the matter. The rabbi's handkerchief apparently serves much the same role as the Bible in the Christian legal tradition—witnesses and confessors place their hands on the handkerchief to swear to the truth of their testimony.

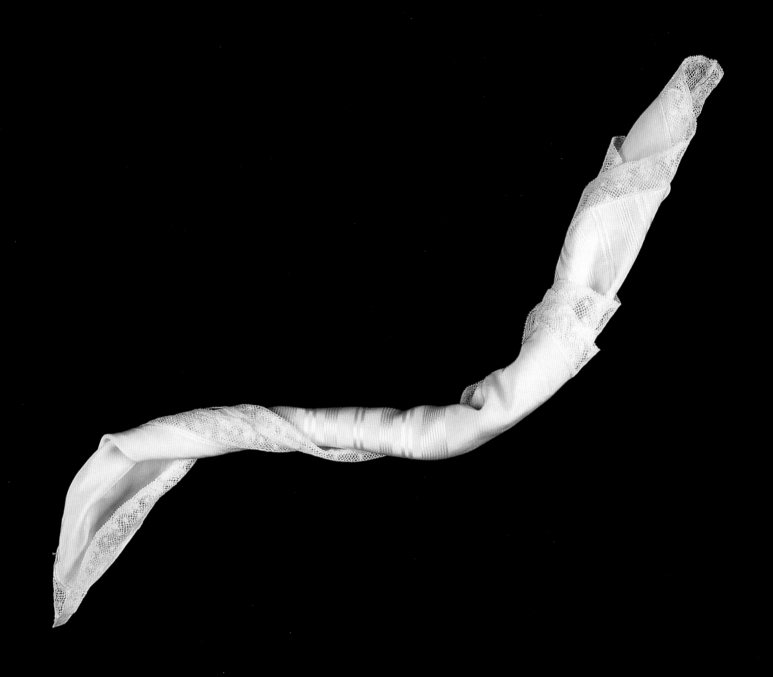

1920s, France, 16¼" x 17", silk.
A very fancy hanky to be used *only* for once-in-a-lifetime occasions.

The Handkerchief
AS STAGE PROP

For stage divas of the 1920s and '30s, large, elegant handkerchiefs replaced the smaller ones popularized by Jenny Lind and other famous singers of the early 1900s. The diva, in a stunning gown standing by the grand piano, a handkerchief pinched with both hands—symbol of strong emotion— was a sight concert-goers expected to see until the 1960s, when the more casual fashions of folksingers spread to the concert stage.

For male performers, however, the handkerchief remains an essential part of their stage arsenal. Louis Armstrong, the incomparable singer and trumpeter, used his handkerchiefs on stage in the same extravagant way that the opera star Luciano Pavarotti still uses his—continually mopping his brow and then waving and fluttering the white square during curtain calls.

In 1954, as a graduate student in the theater arts at the University of Minnesota, I was given the assignment of opening up the concert hall for Louis Armstrong and his big band. I was to be his Minnesota hostess and make sure everything ran smoothly for him. I was thrilled. I met him very early on a snowy Sunday afternoon, and he gave me a quick high five, but that was all.

Passing his dressing room, I spied a tall stack of white handkerchiefs. One had fallen to the floor. The temptation was too great for me. I snatched it up and stuffed it in my pocket—a small sin considering the dozens of dime store hankies in the stack. The greater sin, was that I then lost it.

The current world champion handkerchief user among male performers is James Levine, musical director of the New York Metropolitan Opera. Like an athlete, he literally sweats buckets, and in rehearsals uses a bath towel slung over his shoulder. During performances he uses a large handkerchief with discretion. He also has the jackets of his performance suits made of lightweight silk, with not one, but two underarm gussets (large hidden pleats) to aid movement and ventilation.

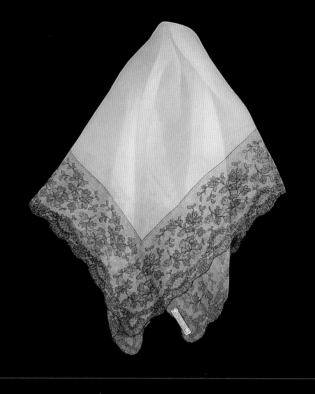

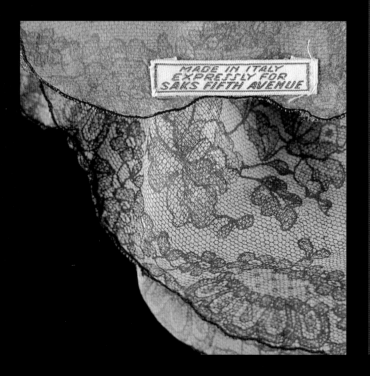

Top left:
1950, 13" diameter, cotton.
A unique hanky, perfectly round, yet roughly finished, the shaky topstitching outlining the whimsical flowers atop the transparent field give it a naïve, yet seductive, air. A marvelous combination of elements.

Top right:
1950s, 26½" x 26½", Italian "chiffon" polyester, trompe l'oeil (trick of the eye) lace design.
However gossamer it may appear, this is a perfect diva's rag—capable of withstanding floods of sweat, tears, and multiple washings. Deliciously transparent and suggestive of lingerie. Hankies are out of fashion with divas today.

Bottom left:
Woven label detail.

DIETRICH CHIFFON

Coco Chanel was a fashion genius, popularizing the bias cut and the sweater and pioneering the wearing of pants, but Marlene Dietrich was not far behind. With her beautifully sculptured face, tweezed eyebrows, and astonishing composure, Dietrich became the quintessence of feminine beauty. She was the first major movie star to wear pantsuits and smartly tailored jackets on and off screen. And this in 1932!

Her hair was soft; her face was soft; her lips were luscious. And though her pants were gracefully cut, there was also something severe about them. In a moment of inspiration, she took a little square of chiffon, approximately four by four inches, and tucked it half-way into her breast pocket. As she moved, the handkerchief undulated in a sexy way—and it drove men wild. Hats off to Dietrich for inventing that enticing little bit of business. I was told by a German acquaintance that she sometimes had her handkerchief sewn into the pocket so she could move freely without fear of it falling out.

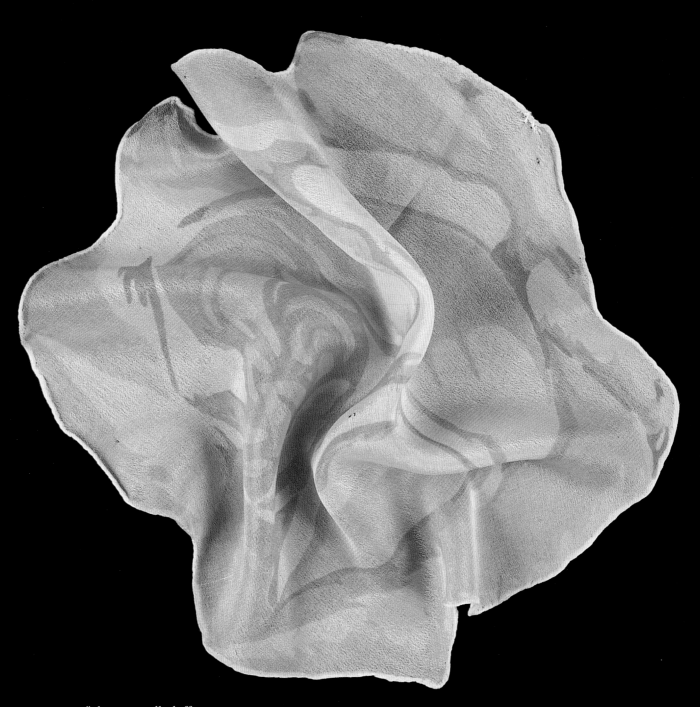

1930s, 11" diameter, silk chiffon.
Unlike most follow-the-form hankies, the border of this unique piece does not follow the outline of the flower so much as it captures the aura of the impressionistic rose. These dainty handkerchiefs were intended to be pinned inside jacket pockets as color accents rather than for actual use.

OLYMPIC HANDKERCHIEF

The 1936 Olympics held in Berlin were a big deal, and the black track star Jesse Owens was America's hero. Despite Adolph Hitler's disapproval of blacks competing, Owens won four gold medals and set records that remained unbroken for twenty-five years. Television was a thing of the future in 1936, so the only chance to see him run came through the grainy black-and-white newsreels that played before the feature film in every movie theater in the land. He was amazing to watch, and the film clips (never long enough) made us all hunger for more glamour, more world status. And they made me, someone with zero interest in sports, want to know more about running.

Soon after Owens wowed the world in Berlin, a short film about him appeared that fed my newborn fascination with running. Among other things, it showed how Owens's coach had modified his running style to increase his speed. Instead of holding his head high and stiff, breast bone pointed to the sky, Owens learned to run in a more relaxed way, allowing his neck to move in rhythm with his stride, so that his head made a nodding motion as he ran. Shown in slow-motion profile, it was a beautiful sight to see.

Now whenever I see the interlocking Olympic rings, I imagine them mirroring the rhythmic motion of Owens's head as he ran to fame. I will never forget those images of him flying ahead of everyone, the enormous crowd going wild.

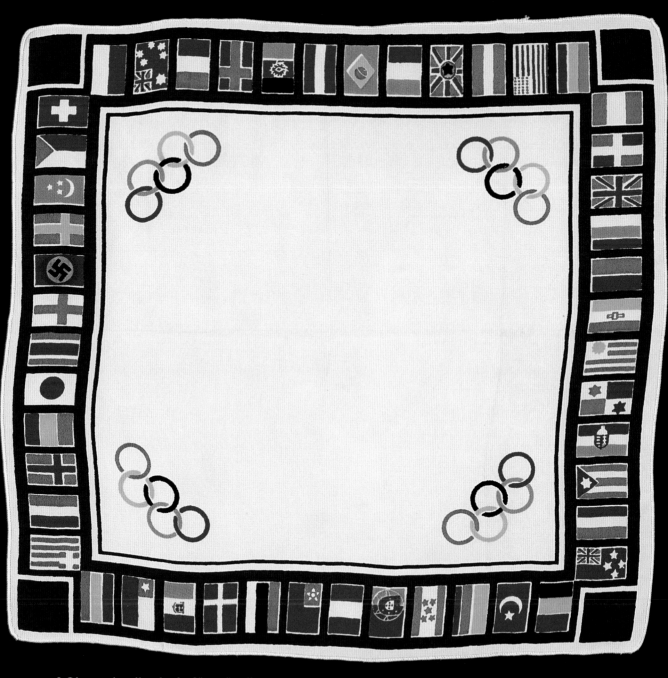

1936 Olympic handkerchief, 16" x 17", silk.
Before Adolph Hitler adopted the swastika (see left border) as the logo of his Nazi party, this universal symbol stood for peace, laughter, joy and good luck. Tibetan farmers placed swastikas above their doorways to ward off evil, as did Irish farmers who referred to the swastika as Brigit's cross. Sadly, the symbol is now considered by many to be synonymous with evil. From the collection of Winifred and Phil Wood.

1936 Olympic handkerchief, 8" x 8", silk.
The five interlocking colored rings of the Olympic
symbol represent the five continents. Blue is for
Europe, yellow is for Asia, black is for Africa, green
is for Australia, and red is for the Americas. The
background of white symbolizes the field of peace
on which the games are to be played. The Olympic
creed stated in 1896 by Baron Pierre de Coubertin,
the founder of the modern games is, "The most
important thing in the Olympic Games is not to
win, but to take part, just as the most important
thing in life is not the triumph, but the struggle."
From the collection of Winifred and Phil Wood.

Top right:
1939 Worlds Fair, 16½" x 18", silk.
To maneuver one's way through the narrow but
friendly passages of Lynn Wiener's Greenwich
Village apartment loft, the shelves laden with
thousands of handkerchiefs and small linens (all
carefully shrouded in clean, well-worn table cloths)
is a thrilling experience. But sitting with her at the
coffee table at the center of her den, viewing her
fabulous collection literally took my breath away.
From the collection of Lynne Wiener.

CORONATION HANDKERCHIEFS

Though we supposedly won our War of
Independence over two hundred years ago,
millions of Americans remain fascinated
with British royalty.

Top right:
1937 George VI Coronation, 11" x 11". silk.
The technology for screening photographic images
onto handkerchiefs was in its infancy in the 1930s,
but for those infatuated with royalty, these were
thrilling mementos featuring "the real things."
From the collection of Winifred and Phil Wood.

Bottom left:
1937 Edward Coronation Handkerchief,
9½" x 10", silk.
This hanky came from the estate of a woman in
Lancaster, Pennsylvania. She was obsessed with
Edward and collected only those things that had
some connection to him. It is said that she had one
in-person interview with him. I wonder what they
talked about? The lipstick smudge on Edward's cheek
suggests she at least kissed the image of her hero.
From the collection of Winifred and Phil Wood.

State Handkerchiefs

Collecting handkerchiefs with the name of the state emblazoned in the corner was a minor craze in the 1930s and '40s. The goal of serious collectors was to get at least one hanky for each of the forty-eight states, no matter how ugly it was. When young women and teenage girls compared their collections, the one who had *all* of the states was the winner.

1940s, 9¾" x 10½", cotton.
Made before the admission of Alaska and Hawaii to the union enlarged the map.

Top left:
1950s, 13½" x 12¾", cotton.
Dogwood blossoms ring the map.

Top right:
1940, 13" x 12¾", cotton.
Unusual combination of two states. From a design perspective, the coast of Rhode Island makes the map much more beautiful than it would have been eastern border.

Bottom left:
Map detail.

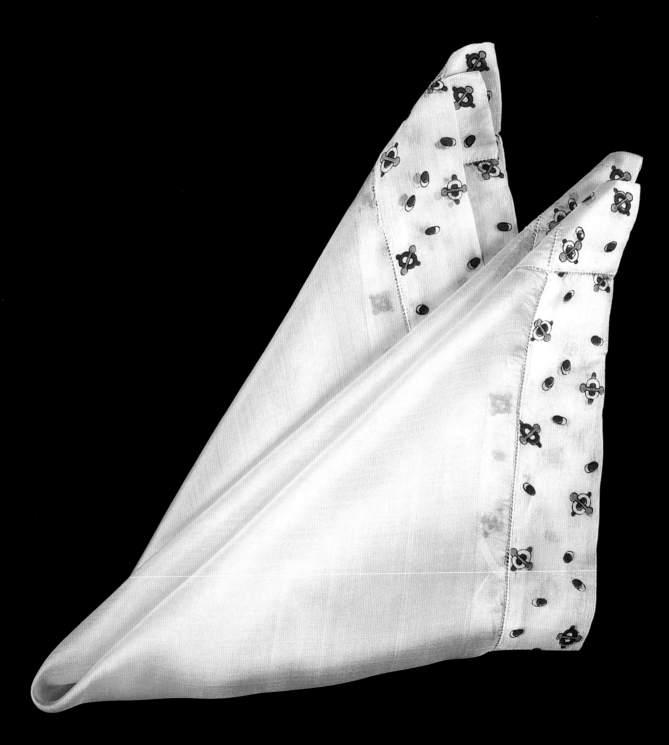

1920, Japan, 18" x 18", lightweight silk dress hanky.
Imagine the sporty effect this elegant piece would make in the pocket of a white linen touring suit.

$\mathcal{S}$ILKS

$\mathcal{M}$agicians call their handkerchiefs silks. "I just got a new set of silks." "I'm working on a tricky silks act." You may have seen a magician take three or four unconnected silk handkerchiefs and stuff them into the top of his closed fist. Then he would tap the closed fist with his free hand and withdraw the handkerchiefs—all of them magically tied together.

But, that's nothing compared with the Dancing Handkerchief routine created by magic-trick inventor Joe Karson in the late 1940s. Imagine a dapper magician borrowing a handkerchief from someone in the audience and tying a knot in one corner. He then stood the handkerchief upright on the stage with the knot at the top, said something equivalent to abracadabra, and the handkerchief started skipping around, flew into a special cabinet, danced inside the cabinet, and then flew back out to continue dancing on the stage. The magician could even leave the scene while the handkerchief danced by itself.

How was this accomplished? Cynics would say that some kind of virtually invisible wire connected the silk to a silent motorized mechanism somewhere on the stage. True believers would simply say, "It's magic!"

1920, Japan, 13" x 14", lightweight silk with "tweed" border.

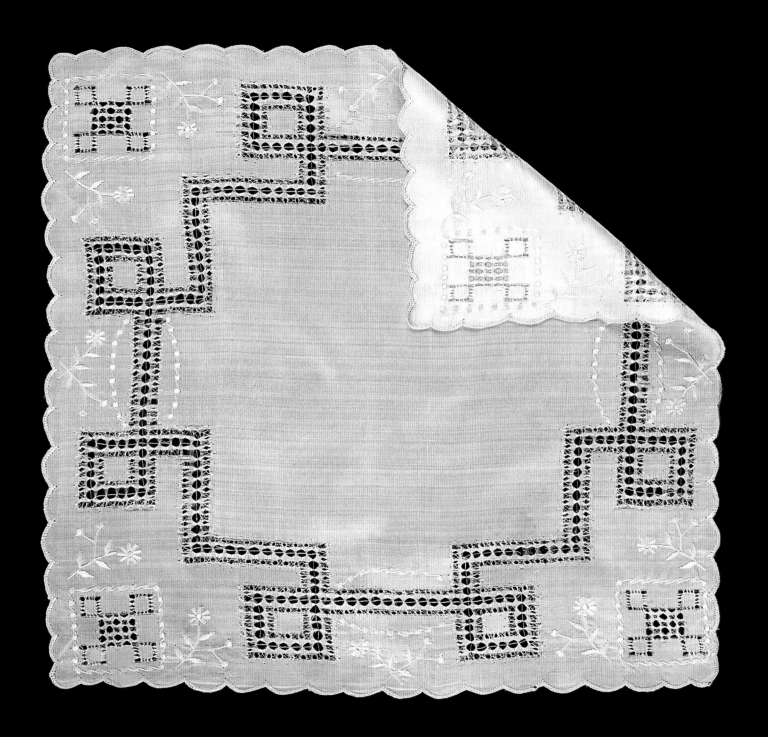

1910, China, 10½" x 11½", natural silk.
Delicate pull work. Chinese style, mimicking Western design.

The Marghab Story

At the turn of the nineteenth century, young Vera Way moved with her family from Iowa to Watertown, South Dakota. Vera grew up to be the belle of the town—a beautiful, elegant, smart, high-thinking Christian Scientist and an accomplished pianist, too. Universally admired for her style and ambition, she resisted for years the persistent entreaties of several eligible swains, finally choosing Emile Marghab, a native of Cyprus, to be her life partner.

In the depths of the Great Depression, Vera and Emile walked the dusty back roads in that remote corner of America's heartland, dreaming a seemingly impossible dream: the creation of a linen company to be centered on the Portuguese island of Madeira in the middle of the Atlantic Ocean. Theirs would be not just *any* linen company but one that would produce the most exquisite linens in the world.

"The continual pursuit of perfection" was their motto, and from 1934 to 1978, the Marghab Company produced what were arguably the finest handkerchiefs and assorted linens made anywhere during the twentieth century. Their linens came from the very best Irish weavers, and their Margandie, a transparent organdy made from Egyptian cotton, was woven and finished for them in Switzerland. Their incomparable embroidery thread came from France, and the embroidery was rendered by the gifted craftswomen of Madeira.

Daisy, 1970, 16¼" x 16½", Egyptian cotton.
The underside of this popular daisy design is almost indistinguishable from the topside—a true measure of its superior quality.

The Marghabs' clientele would eventually include the most wealthy of the wealthy and kings and queens and other royalty from around the world.

Although the rumor persists that Vera designed each piece herself, it was Emile and his brother Theo who did all the designing for the first decade or so of business, with Vera gradually becoming more and more involved in the design process. After Emile's death in 1947, Vera surrounded herself with talented artisans to carry on the then well-established Marghab style and to bring her own artistic ideas to fruition. Marghab designs are by no means cutting edge, but the quality of the finished products is peerless.

So imagine how stunned I was when I first visited the glowing little jewel box of an art museum on the Agricultural campus of South Dakota State University, Brookings, South Dakota, a building wedged between the dairy barn and the Department of Animal Husbandry. The wide prairie stretched out all around me to the far horizons. There, displayed next to the Sioux beadwork and prairie paintings, was this incredible collection of delicate linens—more than 1800 pieces—including a table centerpiece made for the Duchess of Windsor!

When I finally caught my breath, I thought, "Vera did it. Perfection."

Jacaranda Tree, 1960, 8" x 13½", Egyptian cotton.
This guest towel, a wedding present, was the least expensive item in the entire Marghab catalog. I often passed it off as a hanky by holding it folded neatly in half.

Bees, 1980s, 10¾" x 10¾", Egyptian cotton.
A perfectly classic country club hanky—ladies' luncheon and all that.

CLAUDETTE COLBERT

I don't really have a handkerchief story about Claudette Colbert, except to say that whenever I see a handkerchief of silk organza or pineapple linen, especially a delicately elegant one, I think of Claudette Colbert. I was a huge fan of hers. There was something about her unique combination of beauty, physical grace, self-confidence, and smarts that I just loved. I adored her little pointy mouth and soft brown eyes, and those luscious lashes. What a lady and what a babe.

I see her skipping down the steps to her Hollywood swimming pool, wearing a little beige-and-tan tennis outfit: flared shorts made of sharkskin (a sexy shiny rayon material used in the 1940s) and a tailored blouse with the most impossibly perfect padded shoulders—a slightly slapdash but perky handkerchief emerging from her breast pocket and fluttering playfully in the breeze. Delicious!

By the way, pineapple linen is actually made from the leaves of the pineapple plant. This delicate fabric must be cared for properly, or it will not last long. Rough use and exposure to direct sunlight will quickly end its faery life.

Top left:
1935, 11" x 11½", silk organza with appliquéd flower.
A sweet handmade piece, with not a machine stitch
in sight. Possibly made by a dressmaker in the days
when women of means availed themselves regularly
of private seamstresses.

Top right:
1920s, Phillipines, 10" x 10", pineapple linen.
As delicate as pineapple linen may appear, and as
short-lived as it can be if improperly stored, there
is a subtle roughness and crispness to the feel of it:
unique and appealing.

Bottom left:
1890s, 16" x 16", pineapple linen.
The embroidery on this piece was fashioned by
an expert hand. Note the precision of the pull
work detailing.

1950, 15" x 15", cotton with hand-crocheted border.
One of my Aunt Bertha's favorite pieces. Note her careful mending of tiny holes in the fabric. The variegated red and white crocheted edges perfectly mimic the variegated red and pink of the carnations. When at loose ends, Aunt Bertha would turn on the radio, seat herself at the ironing board, and iron handkerchiefs for pleasure.

BORDER DESIGNS

The border of any textile artifact defines the character of the entire work. Each of the handkerchiefs in this section would be greatly diminished without its borders.

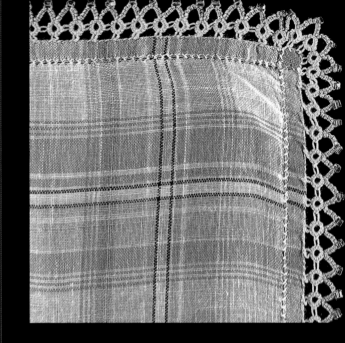

Top right:
1975, 10" x 10½", cotton.
The odd, ornately stitched and beaded border was added by an East Indian embroideress in Berkeley, California. A unique example of border work far transcending the supporting fabric.

Bottom left:
1950s, 11½" x 11½", linen.
The softness of this hanky, due in part to numerous launderings, and the deep pink enhanced by the meticulous border, make it irresistible to those of us who enjoy testing hankies by burying our faces in them.

$\mathscr{P}$ETIT $\mathscr{P}$OINT
REMEMBRANCE

$\mathscr{I}$ found this exquisite petit point handkerchief in my mother's hundred-year-old wooden, satin-lined handkerchief box. The linen is so fine as to be almost transparent. With the handkerchief was a note written in a tiny, cramped, hurried hand signed by Robert Clinton Stauffer, Ensign, United States Naval Reserve.

> *Dear Mrs. Buchta,*
> *Thank you so much for the sweater.*
> *It fits perfectly and I like it very much.*
> *Merry Christmas.*
> *Bob*

Bob was handsome and quiet, an only child, respected by everyone. The handkerchief and card were delivered to my mother by Bob's mother. Bob was killed in World War II a short time later. Mother never used the handkerchief but kept it in memory of him. Although it has turned somewhat gray, it still brings back memories of when young men from our close-knit community—not nameless strangers at a distance—were killed in war. When we got the news of Bob's death, my mother punctuated the event by dabbing the handkerchief with a drop of perfume. I can still recall feeling the sting in my chest when I'd peek into the box and see that she had wrapped it, envelope style, in pale blue tissue paper, to preserve it forever.

Mrs. Stauffer later told my mother that Bob had gone without buying his dinner for two nights to save the money to buy the handkerchief, being at that moment very short on cash.

Top left and right:
1930s, Switzerland, 11" x 11", cotton.
A superior example of petit point. One indication
of excellent petit point is that the back is virtually
indistinguishable from the front.

Bottom left:
1943, 10" x 10½", cotton. Purchased in France in
exchange for a pack of cigarettes during the war
and embroidered by a local French seamstress.
Note perfume stain.

THE RED HANDKERCHIEF

oan Crawford invented the solid red handkerchief. You'll find one in nearly every handkerchief collection. Her creation came from her drive for success coupled with an equally obsessive desire for neatness. I've always felt that Crawford was ahead of her time. She had a personal trainer when that was rare. She ran behind his convertible to "tone up." She finished a facial not with cool water like everyone else but by holding crushed ice to her face for a long time.

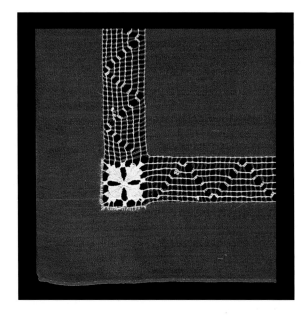

Crawford was relentless about her physical appearance. She had wide hips, for which the admiring designer Adrian "invented" the extended shoulder pads of the 1940s to compensate. She could be haughty and also down-to-earth salesgirl charming. She was a major force in the movie industry.

The story goes that during a high-profile dinner with her producer at a Hollywood hotspot, while prettying up for a moment, she cleaned her lipsticked mouth with her white handkerchief. For her, those red smudges on that field of white were disastrous— a colossal embarrassment! The next day she asked her seamstress to make her a red handkerchief, and soon every woman had to have one.

1950s, China, 15" x 15", cotton.
The intricate drawn work employing an uneven pattern invigorates the border. A perfect lipstick hanky.

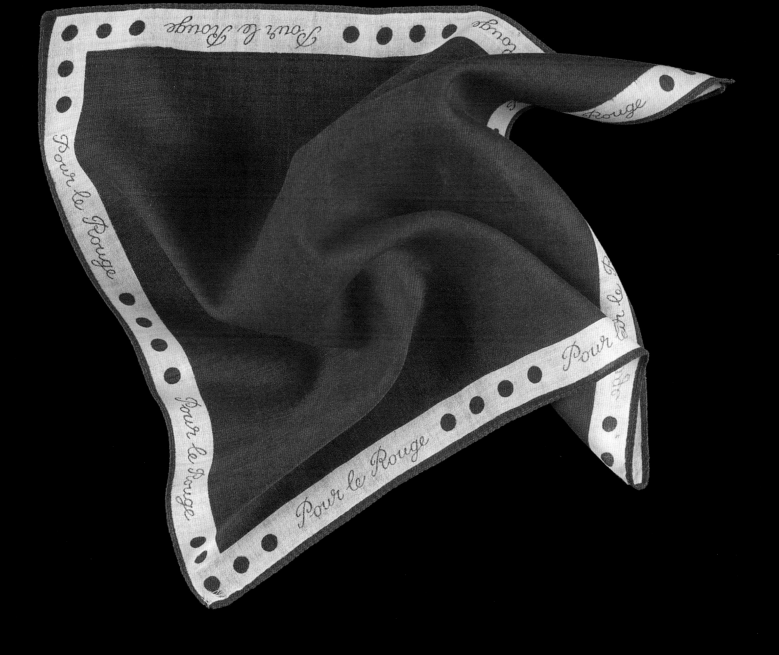

1950, France, 9½" x 10", cotton, machine hemmed.
A French version of an American invention.

JEANETTE MCDONALD

This handkerchief was given to me by a pal who grew up next door to Jeanette McDonald. She bought it at a quiet little estate sale after McDonald's death and she kept it for years as a reminder to keep her life in balance—as McDonald had not.

One day, many years before, my friend had met the famous actress on the quiet roads of Brentwood, McDonald on her horse, my friend, then fourteen, on foot.

"Oh Miss McDonald, I hope when I grow up I'll be as famous as you are," my friend gushed.

"My dear," she replied, "I hope you never have to work as hard as I have."

Then the actress wiped a tear from her eye with a handkerchief that very well might have been this one, though we'll never know.

A four-handkerchief novella.

—Andrea Chambers, from her review of Eric Segal's *Love Story*

1938, 11" x 12", cotton.
Rich browns were very popular in the late 1930s. The jagged edged flowers and the stylized leaves of this elegant piece reflect the influences Modern Art and the growing sophistication of commercial art design. The colors make it a perfect choice for a Hollywood equestrian.

FORBIDDEN LINEN

In the 1950s and into the early 1960s, many young girls adored handkerchiefs. My friend Judith lived in Buffalo, New York, at a time when some schools required special handkerchief pockets on blouses as part of the school uniform.

By the age of twelve, Judith was obsessed with handkerchiefs. Whenever her mother was out, she would sneak into her mother's bedroom, open the top drawer of the dresser—a dark chevron with delicate gold trim—and take out every single handkerchief. She'd place them on the bed in an orderly fashion: blues with blues, pinks with pinks, yellows with yellows, and whites all together. She would flip them this way and that, pretending to be Elizabeth Taylor playing with her jewels, imagining herself to be rich and stylish. Then she'd carefully fold them and put them away.

One day Judith couldn't resist the temptation to borrow one of her mother's scores of handkerchiefs, but within the week her mother discovered it was missing, and there was hell to pay.

Many years later, a mother herself, Judith was sorting her large collection of handkerchiefs, arranging them on her bed just as she had done with her mother's handkerchiefs, when she was struck with what a beautiful quilt they would make. And that's how she came to make her first handkerchief quilt.

1940, cotton, 13½" x 13½".
This blurry blend of burgundies around a white center would be a lovely piece in itself, but the flamboyant monogrammed F with its thick white top stitching creates a striking illusion of depth.

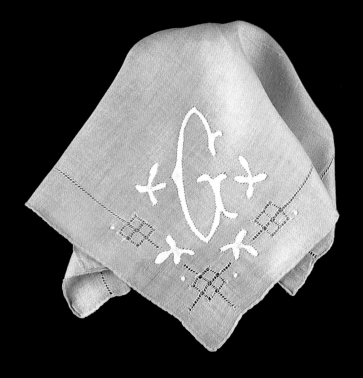

Top left:
1940, 11½" x 12", cotton.
The sharply contrasting red and black halves joined
by the top stitched letter give this piece a dramatic,
three-dimensional feel.

Top right:
1940, 11½" x 11½", cotton, appliqué and drawn work.

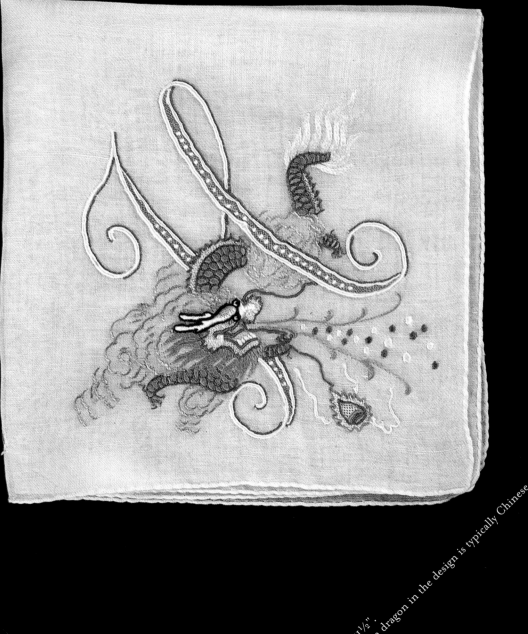

FLORA'S FAMOUS HANDKERCHIEF

Given to me by a chef, this handkerchief is an exact replica of the one purchased by Flora Fouquet for a special trip through France. She lived in a small village and was preparing to celebrate her twenty-fifth wedding anniversary in a very special way. The handkerchief was much more than a pretty convenience; it was a map for an automobile excursion—an itinerary of some of the high-profile restaurants in France. The popular social game was to dine well and expensively at as many of these restaurants as possible, and have each chef autograph the appropriate square on the handkerchief. This show-off piece would prove you had money enough to make the trip and you had culinary taste, too. An honor badge of middle-class French women of the 1950s, this little piece of cloth would greatly increase your standing in the community.

Flora was smart, stout, and persistent. She and her husband, Paul Bernard, cleaned and polished their old Peugeot until it gleamed, and then they made sure to depart on Sunday just after Mass so everyone would see them leaving. The trip proceeded flawlessly; the weather was beautiful. They drove and drove and ate and ate. The chefs were all happy to sign. Flora tucked the handkerchief into her bosom each night, sleeping in her brassiere to ensure the precious hanky's safety. But somehow, upon their return, it was missing.

Anguished and forced to use the only phone in town—a public one outside the post office—she called the last three restaurants they'd visited. Cheeks flaming, Flora made her agonized pleas to various maître d's, all in earshot of everyone passing by and everyone inside the post office. She knew her tragedy would be the talk of the town for weeks.

Flora never found her handkerchief, but Bernard replaced it with a brand new one. When I got it, the handkerchief was pristine, crisp, and professionally folded, which told me it had never been used. I have never used it either for fear of starting a losing curse.

Guide Gastronomique

AIX-EN-PROVENCE
VENDÔME
- LOUP FLAMBÉ AU FENOUIL
- AGNEAU DES BAUX

AIX-LES-BAINS
QUATRE-VALETS
- OMBLE CHEVALIER NANTUA
- FEUILLETÉ AU RIS DE VEAU

ANNECY CHAVOIRE
PAVILLON ERMITAGE
- OMBLE HOLLANDAISE
- POULET GRILLÉ À LA DIABLE

AU COL DE LA LUÈRE PRÈS DE LYON
MÈRE BRAZIER
- QUENELLES BELLE AURORE
- POULET GRILLÉ BÉARNAISE

AUTUN S.&L.
ST-LOUIS
- ÉCREVISSES À LA CRÈME
- POULET À LA ROMAINE

AVALLON YONNE
HÔTEL DE LA POSTE
- TRUITE FOURRÉE AU FUMET DE MEURSAULT
- POULET DE BRESSE EN CIVET

BORDEAUX
CHAPON FIN
- FILETS DE SOLE MAISON
- CÈPES BORDELAISE

BOUGIVAL S.&O.
COQ HARDY
- GRATIN DE HOMARD
- BRIOCHE BRILLAT-SAVARIN

CHATELLERAULT
FAISAN
- TERRINE DE VOLAILLE TRUFFÉE
- CANARD À L'ORANGE

DONNEMARIE S.&M.
AUBERGE DU MONTOIS
- PÂTÉ D'ANGUILLES
- TERRINE DE FOIES DE VOLAILLE

FEURS LOIRE
CHAPEAU ROUGE
- GRENOUILLES
- MOUSSELINE DE BROCHET

HÉDÉ I.&V.
VIEUX MOULIN
- HUÎTRES FOURRÉES
- HOMARD CÔTE D'ÉMERAUDE

LAMASTRE ARDÈCHE
MIDI
- PAIN D'ÉCREVISSES
- POULARDE EN VESSIE

LES BAUX B.-DU-R.
BAUMANIÈRE
- ROUGET EN PAPILLOTE
- PINTADEAU À LA BROCHE

LES PONTS-NEUFS C-DU-N.
LORAND-BARRE
- HOMARD GRILLÉ
- POULARDE COCOTTE

LILLE
À L'HUÎTRIÈRE
- PRODUITS DE LA MER

LOUÉ SARTHE
RICORDEAU
- TERRINE MAISON
- POULET POÊLÉ AUX MORILLES

LYON
LE MOLIÈRE
- LANGOUSTE MAISON
- POULET DE BRESSE AU CHAMPAGNE

MARSEILLE
CAMPA
- BOUILLABAISSE
- ROUGET GRILLÉ

MONTBARD CÔTE D'OR
HÔTEL DE LA GARE
- TRUITE «CAPRICE DE BUFFON»
- JAMBON BRAISÉ AU CHAMBERTIN

MONTE CARLO
HÔTEL DE PARIS
- OMELETTE SOUFFLÉE
- DAURADE À LA PÊCHEUR
- POIRE GISMONDA

MOUGINS ALPES-MAR.
LA MUSARDE
- FILET DE BŒUF GRILLÉ
- VOLAILLE MUSARDE

NICE
ST. MORITZ
- GRATIN DE FILETS DE SOLE AU CHAMPAGNE
- GÂTEAU SOUFFLÉ FEUILLETÉ

ORLÉANS
AUBERGE ST. JACQUES
- BROCHET DE LOIRE
- COQ AU VIN DE CHINON

PARIS
LAPÉROUSE
- CANETON COLETTE
- ROGNONS DE VEAU

PÉROUGES AIN
OSTELLERIE VIEUX PÉROUGES
- VOLAILLE DE BRESSE
- GALETTE PÉROUGIENNE

POUILLY-SUR-LOIRE
ESPÉRANCE
- QUENELLES DE BROCHET
- COQ AU VIN BLANC

RIOM P.-DE-D.
LE PAILLARET
- HOMARD MAISON
- POULET MAISON

ROQUEFORT AVEY RON
GRAND HOTEL
- FEUILLETÉ ROQUEFORTAIS
- TRUITE AUX AMANDES

SAULIEU
CÔTE D'OR
- TERRINE AU CHAMBERTIN
- JAMBON DU MORVAN AU GRATIN

SENS YONNE
PARIS ET POSTE
- ESCARGOTS MAISON
- CANARD AUX POMMARD

ST. TROPEZ
LEI MOUSCARDINS
- LANGOUSTE GRILLÉE AUX HERBES
- CHAPON RIZ PILAFF

STRASBOURG
VALENTIN SORG
- FOIE GRAS CHAUD
- COQ AU RIESLING

TALLOIRES H.-SAVOIE
AUBERGE DU PÈRE BISE
- OMBLE CHEV AU PORTO
- POULARDE DE BRESSE À L'ESTRAGON

THOISSEY AIN
CHAPON FIN
- GRENOUILLES SAUTÉES FINES HERBES
- CHAPON À LA CRÈME

TÔTES S-INF
CYGNE
- LANGOUSTE À LA NEWBURG
- POULET MAISON

VALENCE DRÔME
PIC
- CHAUSSON AUX TRUFFES
- GRATIN DE QUEUES D'ÉCREVISSES

VIENNE ISÈRE
PYRAMIDE "POINT"
- TRUITE FARCIE AU PORTO
- VOLAILLE À LA CRÈME

VILLENEUVE LAN-DES
VOYAGEURS
- FOIE GRAS
- ÉCREVISSES

de la France

DESSIN DÉPOSÉ

1950s, France, 13¼" x 13¼", cotton, hand-rolled hem.

"I weep for you," the Walrus said:
"I deeply sympathize."
With sobs and tears he sorted out
Those of the largest size,
Holding his pocket handkerchief
Before his streaming eyes.

—Lewis Carroll, from
The Walrus and the Carpenter

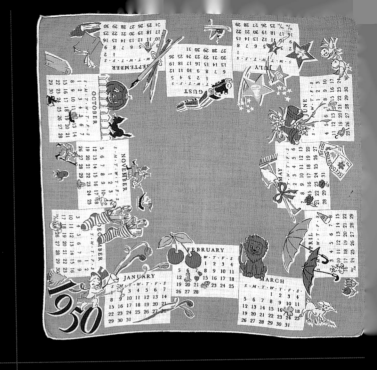

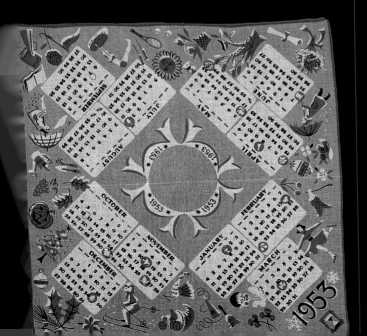

Top right:
1950, 13" x 12¼", cotton.
Calendar hankies were a favorite Christmas gift to
give—something to celebrate the coming new year.
However, they are not particularly useful as calendars
go and were sold as novelty items.

Bottom left:
1953, 13" x 13½", cotton.

1950s, 13" x 13", cotton.
The layout of this hanky is a far cry from the classical floral designs that dominated handkerchief design before World War II. The 1950s were the beginning of the Nuclear Age, the age when Facts, Science, and Pragmatism superseded Art and Philosophy. This calorie chart is not particularly accurate. Note the calorie count for the box of bon bons.

1960s, 13⅓" x 12¾" , cotton.
A fine example of graphic art style—the use of parallel lines to delineate the flowers is slightly unusual.

BEAUTIFUL BLUES

Falling between green and violet on the color spectrum, predominantly blue handkerchiefs stand out in any collection—oceanic, ethereal, and strong—the color of constancy.

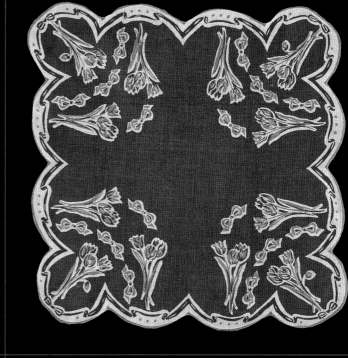

Top right:
1940, 12½" x 12½", cotton.
The natural depth imparted by this rich royal blue, underlying the white shadowing around the flowers and the lighter blue ribbons, give this piece its electric vibrancy. The Puerto Rican seamstress had the extra difficulty of rendering the curved border, though she gained no extra pay for her effort since she was paid by the piece.

Bottom left:
1950s, France, 11¼" x 12¼".
What at first glance seems to be merely a pretty piece reminiscent of Tammis Keefe, this hanky actually tells a bittersweet tale. It unfolds from the top left-hand corner and continues as if you are reading a page from a book. The photographer, obviously in love with his model, becomes so involved with his picture taking that he fails to see her being swept away by the romantic horseman, though the whole sad affair is captured on film.

Look Into the Sun

During World War II, American women professionals did not flaunt big wardrobes—all their dresses and suits were subdued aquas, tans, browns, perhaps dark purple. Shirtwaist dresses, with breast pockets on the left, fabric-covered belts and buckles, and pleated skirts of a sensible length, were very popular. Little or no makeup was the style in those somber times, at least at our modest Minnesota high school.

When it came to economy of dress, Miss Herschenberger, my math teacher, was the undisputed champion. She had three outfits, total: two well-worn rayon shirtwaist dresses, one black, the other maroon, and a tan tweed suit worn with a white bow blouse. She rotated them regularly, though the maroon dress was her favorite. She had one handkerchief, a dime-store item that nicely blended with all *three* outifts. It was neatly folded and placed in the left breast pocket of whichever outfit she was wearing. She never removed the handkerchief from this pocket, but she did use it in a singular and fascinating way.

Before I reveal how she used this handkerchief, let me assure you that in all other ways Miss Herschenberger was the soul of propriety—a solid, reasonable woman and the best math teacher I ever had.

Every once in a while, usually during a quiet study period, she would cross the room to the south-facing window, squint up at the sun, and pull at her handkerchief with the tips of her fingers. Then she would say in a ringing, commanding voice, "I am the only one who can look into the sun."

Believe it or not, we never laughed at her. We never even let on that we had heard her. But we lived for those moments. Perhaps she did, too. As strange as this may sound, the way in which she made her pronouncement—with such strength and confidence—was empowering. There by the window, gazing proudly at the sun, her fingers touching her handkerchief and also her heart, Miss Herschenberger taught us a most important lesson: that it was perfectly acceptable to be unique; we didn't have to be anyone but ourselves. That was a great gift for us to take into the world.

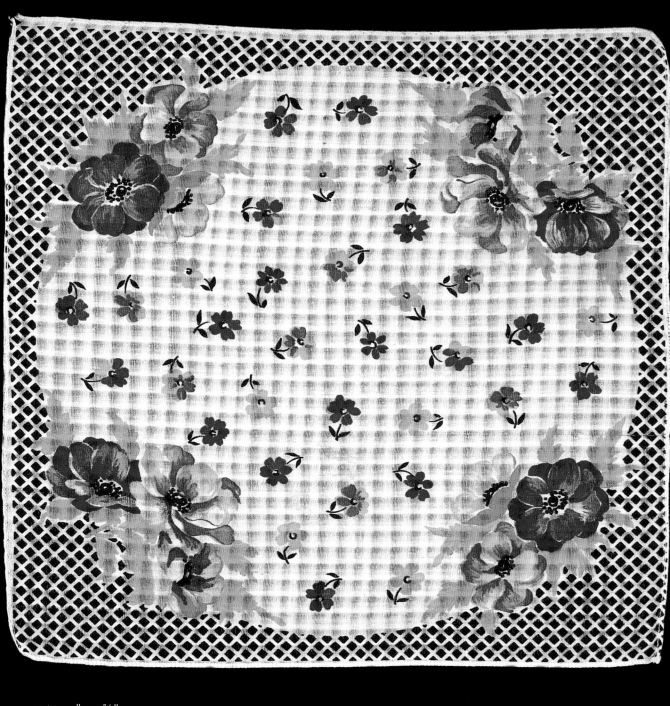

1940, 11" x 11¾", cotton.
Miss Herschenberger's hanky. An upscale dime store purchase, this hanky with its hand rolled hem, may have cost as
much as a dime. The black checks framing the flowers add dignity to this piece.

Sail Away

In December of 1954, I set sail from New York on an army transport ship bound for Europe. I had been assigned to a U.S. Army Special Services position, and I had no idea how things were going to be when I got to Germany. As the big ship picked up speed, I began to feel panicky, and I understood the word *heartsick* for the first time. As we passed under the lovely, strong arms of the Statue of Liberty, I thought, "Oh, no. I'm going the wrong way."

The beautiful goddess of liberty also reminded me that I'd bought a special green handkerchief, designed by the legendary Tammis Keefe, to match what I thought was going to be my fashionably khaki uniform. Alas, our Special Services uniforms turned out to be a soft Air Force blue. The effect of my handkerchief wouldn't be what I'd hoped it would be.

I watched our Lady disappear into the fog and pocketed my fears and my silly pride along with the handkerchief.

NEW YORK ★ NEW YORK ★ NEW YORK

STATUE OF LIBERTY

STATUE OF LIBERTY

NEW YORK ★ NEW YORK

1953, 13½" x 12½", cotton.

This is an unusual Tammis Keefe design for a number of reasons: It is a picture of a place rather than a grouping of similar objects; the figure of the Statue of Liberty is much larger than Tammis usually made things; and the colors are brilliantly offbeat for such a patriotic theme, giving credence to those who feel Tammis Keefe was a colorist first and foremost

RENATA'S COLLECTION

After a lifetime of collecting a wide range of handkerchiefs, European-born Renata Polt focused her search on unique 1950s-style pieces from France and Switzerland. Presented here are some select pieces from her collection.

Top right:
1980s, France, 11½" x 12", cotton.
The blank space on the telegram suggest that this hanky was to be personalized with embroidery by the seller or the purchaser. It is delicious to put one's own "mark" on a gift.

Bottom left:
1960s, 12" x 13", France, cotton.
Unique, daring, eye candy. The contrast of the black and white kiosk and the brilliant bursts of colors, plus the wonderful use of perspective and shadows, make this piece stunningly cinematic.

2000, France, 12 3/4" x 13", silk, machine hemmed.
This luscious handkerchief is the one I wore, dangling provocatively from the pocket of my carefully chosen plaid shirt,
on the day I made the deal to create *Hanky Panky* for Ten Speed Press.

1950s, Switzerland, 10" x 10¼", cotton.
A whimsical piece, yet full of Swiss precision and detail. An American souvenir hanky of this sort would undoubtedly bear the names of each of the landmarks shown, but for the Swiss the identities of these places are too obvious to name.

Vivez, si m'en croyez, n'attendez à demain
Cueillez dès aujourd'hui les roses de la vie

Pierre de RONSARD

1935, France, 12" x 11", cotton.
The lines of the poem by Pierre de Ronsard translate to "Live, believe in me, don't wait till tomorrow. Gather the roses of Life today." Ronsard (1524-1585) was called *"le prince des poètes, le poète de princes."* He was a great favorite of European royalty, and it is recorded that Queen Elizabeth I of England sent him a large diamond.

Cigar Box Array

When I was mad for antiques in the 1980s and '90s, I ran across a most unusual secondhand store in a very small, dusty town in the Midwest. I bought a quilt that day, and a bucket to use as a wastebasket. I also found a wooden cigar box full of handkerchiefs. I was trying to save money, so I sat outside on the steps of the shop, unfolding one handkerchief after the other, carefully examining each one, trying to decide which to buy. There was a whole panoply of handkerchiefs—some very worn ones, some quite nice, and some just a little bit nice. As I sat there, the proprietor stood over me and said, "Well, why don't you buy the whole box? It's only a dollar." Feeling rather foolish, I thought, 'Why not, of course.'

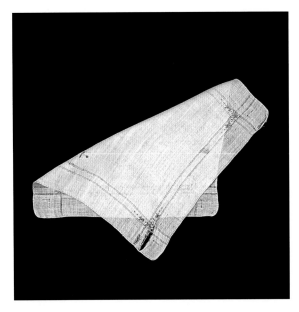 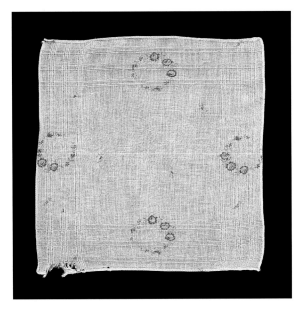

Left: 1930s, 9" x 9", cotton, hand-embroidered details.
Right: 1930s, 10¼" x 10¼" , cotton. The ravaged edges of this piece speak volumes about its owner's poverty.

When I got home, I leafed through the collection very slowly. The first handkerchief had obviously been pressed and used a great deal. It had a poignant hole in the corner where its owner—I was sure the handkerchiefs belonged to a woman—had repeatedly clamped her two fingers. I thought, 'This woman didn't have any money. It was the Depression.'

Another contained the signature colors of 1933–1935: brown, a pallid orange, and that medium pea green now known as Depression Green. It had the feel and look of a panel cut from the skirt of a housedress and hemmed inappropriately with a blanket stitch; the stitching at the edges was far too heavy for the weight of the handkerchief. A simple rolled hem would have been more appropriate. This woman lacked not only money but also experience in embroidery.

The handkerchief at the bottom of the box was the one that really tugged at my heart. It was white with sprigs of blue and pink, really very pretty, and I thought, "Ah, here's her Sunday go-to-church-meetin' handkerchief." Then I picked it up. It was made of curtain material, marquisette, as nonabsorbent as a piece of steel screening, laboriously hemmed, the fabric so stiff that she could hardly turn it over to make a rolled hem. It seemed obvious to me that this was the handkerchief she pulled out on Sunday to dramatically wipe her eyes or pat her cheeks—but all for show, because it was not a functional handkerchief. Think of the pain of repressed pride in her sleight of hand.

1930s, 11¾" x 12¼", cotton.
This may have been a Mother's Day gift from the daughter using a blanket stitch to finish the edges. A beginner's stitch, the blanket stitch is so called because it is commonly used to seal the edges of blankets.

1930s, 11½" x 12", marquisette.
This is the only hanky in the cigar box that appeared fresh and clean. Made from marquisette—a tough, shimmering organdy substitute more commonly used for curtains, it was also used for formal wear. Jackie Kennedy's first debutante gown was made of marquisette and bought "off the rack."

Marilyn Sprague

Marilyn Sprague (Ashworth, Ainsley, Smithers) is a fictional young lady, but I've met, known, and admired (loathed, hated, and sneered at) her all my life. Everything about her is sweet, salubrious, smooth, balanced, secure, and shining. Her fingernails are always perfect—glowing with a pale natural flesh color. Even when she lowers herself to paint her nails red, they are still perfect without chips. She is a Breck Girl, even if she's a brunette (though she's almost always a blond in the ads, with easy-to-care-for hair). She drives a beige convertible that her father gave her when she went off to Stanford or its East Coast equivalent.

She owns at least five pale-hued cashmere sweater sets, neatly nestled in tissue paper in her cedar-scented dresser drawer. She handles her checkbook without a hitch and always has plenty of cash in her purse. She never hurries. She plays bridge beautifully. She is a truly lovely, sweet person who knows how to be a good friend, and I love to be with her, absorbing all her sense of refinement and quiet and amplitude. When I'm not doting on her, I hate her. Yet I wish I could be just like her.

The handkerchief here is typical of the kind that mothers of the Marilyn Spragues of this world, circa 1935–60 sent off with their daughters to college. Note the neat stitches nailing down, as it were, Marilyn Sprague's name, such care suggesting that the loss of the hanky to some stranger would be tantamount to a loss of Marilyn Sprague's honor. The Marilyn Spragues of the world, and their mothers and fathers, have all but vanished from the American landscape, though remnants remain in various upscale suburban neighborhoods.

Marilyn Sprague went off to college with dozens of these handkerchiefs—all chosen with great care to harmonize with her sweater sets.

MARILYNN SPRAGUE

1950–60s, 12½" x 13", cotton.
A dime store purchase, probably one of a dozen identical pieces, the fabric equivalent of a business card.

THE DANCING DOCTOR

Aunt Alverta—Auntie Al—was a meticulous, careful, and wholesomely stylish dresser. I adored every inch of her well-heeled, ample self. I recall a day in 1972 when she came into her dining room neatly coifed and wearing her best Sunday suit, a well-pressed, delicate aqua wool crepe, with a cream-colored bow blouse embellished with aquamarine jewelry scattered here and there. She plumped down her purse on the gleaming table, along with a slightly crumpled white tatted handkerchief, and started to make after-church coffee, her usual routine.

"Ah," I asked, "is that the famous hankie, the one that Dr. Somkin danced with?"

"That's the one," she said exuberantly. "And this is the very suit I was wearing the day I went to see him."

Women of her class and generation dressed up to go to the doctor. In 1971, Auntie Al had been tested for cancer, and when she went to get the results of her biopsy, she wore a "foundation garment" (a girdle, covering the entire torso), a lightweight "dress shield" fastening underneath the breasts protecting the armpit area of the blouse, hosiery attached by garters, a full slip, jewelry, and all the rest. Nails were buffed or painted a soft pink. Rosy cheeked, subtly perfumed, she radiated salubrious crispness and Quality.

Dr. Somkin, by contrast, had become enamored of the hippie look. His long, frizzy curls rested on an open shirt, and his well-kept toes peeked through his sandals. Despite appearances, he was a respected M.D. Most of all, he was *clean,* my aunt reported again and again in guarded defense, and she approved. After she heard the good news, she wept, and from her purse—a boxy affair, known as a Queen Elizabeth #2, smelling deliciously of its leather lining—she picked out this pristine handkerchief (made by Aunt Della May), with which she dabbed at the happy tears spilling from her eyes.

Dr. Somkin sped across the examining room, sandals flapping, curls bouncing, and grabbed the handkerchief, crying, "Oh, Mrs. Herrmann, I've always wanted a patient who used a handkerchief. A lady! A real lady!" And he danced away, waving this lacy perfection back and forth like a cheerleader. I often thought I should frame the famous rag, and now I have.

1950, 11½" x 11½", cotton.
The extra flourishes in this lovely tatting reflect my Aunt Della Mae's exuberant, bubbly personality. Nothing she did was ordinary or reserved. When everyone else's porch ceiling was painted sky blue, Aunt Della Mae's was pink. Note: This beautifully tatted handkerchief is consistent and delicate; and holes are all precisely the same diameter, the mark of a truly careful and skilled needlewoman.

1920s, 28" x 18", cotton.
Made from three identical hankies, there is most definitely a front and a back to this apron. The backside identifies the seamstress as inexperienced (or in a tremendous hurry) but the design is clever and alluring. Given its daintiness, this was a party apron and not for heavy kitchen use.

Boathouse Hanky Apron

In 1968, Margaret Meredith Spencer—a striking beauty with long brown hair—came to San Francisco to experience the great hippie happening centered in the Haight Ashbury district. Her people, sound Omaha folk, thought she was coming out to attend law school at the University of California. Instead, she made that other scene, and moments after her arrival in San Francisco, she appeared in a full-length, paisley granny gown, scented with patchouli oil, and took her place in the parade of pleasure seekers, social revolutionaries, and wide-eyed tourists.

Soon she encountered Michael, a delightfully creative émigré from Santa Cruz. As far as Margaret Meredith was concerned, it was kismet. During a Clothes-Off Swimming Happening in a Sausalito boathouse, she cornered Michael and made her intentions clear. She presented her lips. He leaned to kiss her—the air was hot. Suddenly he withdrew. Margaret Meredith was distraught. The moment was gone, but not for long.

The next morning, as Michael sat idly sipping kefir and leafing through the *Haight Ashbury Flash*, Margaret Meredith appeared and started doing the dishes. She wore this charming pink apron—fashioned from three handkerchiefs—and nothing else. He was helpless. They married six years later.

Oh hail to the handkerchief—an article of infinite uses.

1930s, 12½" x 12½", cotton.
Using a classic 1930s color scheme, this eight-sided umbrella brilliantly combines form, colors, and subtle elements of romance.

FOLLOW THE FORM

Rarely manufactured today, handkerchiefs
en silhouette are emblematic of the astonishing
variety of shapes and styles available
during the last Golden Age
of hankies—the 1930s and 40s.

Top right:
1940s, 13" x 13", rayon.
A fancy hanky for dressy occasions—a show piece only.
This one looks good no matter how you clutch it,
dangle it, or fold it into a pocket.

Bottom left:
1940s, 15" x 15", cotton.
Without realizing it, I have acquired not one or two,
but several giant purple pansy hankies over the years.
This one is particularly bold and dramatic. Gigantic
oversized flowers were all the rage in handkerchief
designs of the 1930s and 1940s, preceding Georgia
O'Keeffe's sensual flower paintings.

$\mathcal{V}$ERA

$\mathcal{V}$era Salaff Neumann, her last name virtually unknown to her millions of admirers—was easily the most famous designer of scarves in the world from the late 1940s through the early 1960s, surpassing Echo, Schiaparelli, and Chanel in popularity. Women in all walks of life coveted her whimsical, colorful, elegant creations. Marilyn Monroe, Queen Elizabeth, and anybody who was anybody—or anybody who wanted to be somebody—wore Vera scarves.

Vera, an abstract painter, founded the company called Vera with her husband in 1946. Perhaps because her stylish imagery became so ubiquitous on scarves, handkerchiefs, wallpaper, and fabrics, she was never given much credit as a "serious" artist, though she never considered herself anything less.

In the 1940s, it was extremely important for women of my class and station to be supremely well groomed. Shoes, handbag, belt, and gloves had to match. The seams of stockings had to be straight. The path to being considered chic was narrow, even brittle, in its requirements. One thing we could cling to was the designer label. It was just beginning to emerge as a fashion phenomenon and was comforting for the socially insecure. The designer's stamp of approval meant that no actual judgment was required, only money and knowing the right thing to buy. The Vera label on a scarf or handkerchief was like a ticket to the ball. You bought it; you got in.

In my sophomore year of high school, I wanted badly to make a grand appearance at the big, annual mother-daughter tea. I borrowed a simple, pale yellow wool crepe dress from a grown-up neighbor. It was a little worn looking across the neck and shoulders, but I had saved my allowance to buy a pale yellow, gold, and tan Vera scarf that could be draped over the neck and shoulder to hide everything. The scarf design was bright and bold and stylish. I was thrilled.

I dressed with care, but fussed with the scarf too long. Moments before we were supposed to leave for the big event, I heard a sickening ripping sound. The left armhole of the dress had given way, exposing thick underarm hair. I had not yet been given permission by my mother to shave, and I can still feel the panic that gripped me. Arms crossed, pacing around my room, I held myself back from hysteria until I realized that all I had to do was keep my left arm glued to my side during the tea and lift my cup with my right. I reminded myself of the dance I'd gone to the year before with a pal of mine. He was a bit shorter than I, so I wore a full, stiff taffeta skirt and bent my knees a bit so I would not tower over him. We danced happily together the entire evening. True, my knees ached the next day, but I didn't mind.

Since I'd suffered for fashion before, I could do it again. And it worked! I looked great at the tea and quickly gave up trying to pick up a cookie. No one noticed anything amiss with my outfit and the Vera scarf was a big hit.

I mended the dress that night and returned it the next day. I congratulated myself on being grown-up, devious, glamorous, and, most of all, fashionable.

1960s, 10¼" x 10½", cotton.
Vera was synonymous with scarves, so a true handkerchief by her is a rare find. This lovely artifact owes a great deal to the abstract paintings of Piet Mondrian who spent his last years in New York in the early 1940s where Vera was a practicing studio artist as well as a fabric designer. From the collection of Lynne Wiener.

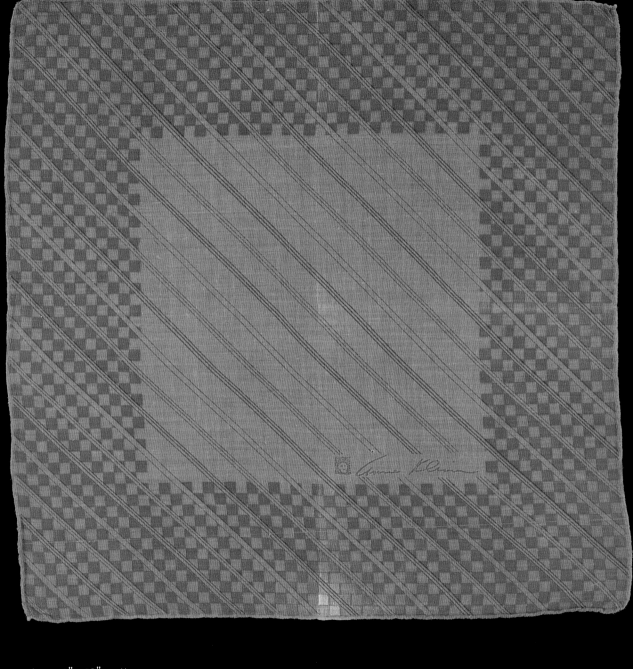

1970s, 13" x 13", cotton.
It is no accident that most of Anne Klein's hankies were perfectly square and employed squares and straight edges as the primary elements of her design. Her pieces were intended to be elegant complements to her clothing, and to be, well, square. As in conservative.

ANNE KLEIN DESIGNS

Enamored of all things classical, Klein's conservative elegance appealed to everybody—old money and New Age alike.

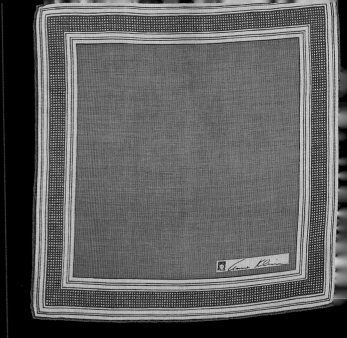

Top right:
1970s, 13" x 13", cotton.
Intentionally non-illustrative, the deep, muted orange that dominates both these pieces is what they are all about—a touch of solid color to accent her highly controlled elegance.

Bottom left:
Signature detail.

WHAT HANDKERCHIEFS
MAY REVEAL

A stiff and formal business executive, Charles Wilson, head of General Motors in the 1950s, wore a handkerchief showpiece that was not a handkerchief at all. It was a rectangle of cardboard with a piece of cloth folded over the top. It was only for show—a monolithic rail—unforgiving and as strict.

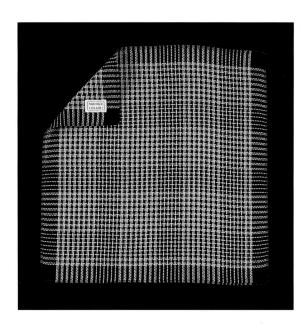

Harry Truman, by contrast, loved to dress up. He adored haberdashery and elegant clothes. In the 1950s, there was a slight distinction between a handkerchief displayed with three points and one folded to show four points. It was a little bit like the number of buttons on the cuff, with more buttons indicating greater elegance and expense. So Truman wore a handkerchief with four *very carefully* folded points, placing it prominently in his shirt pocket, never to be used.

By contrast, Franklin Delano Roosevelt was known to dress casually and stuff handkerchiefs here and there. He used to lie in bed wearing an old cardigan sweater full of holes, instead of a bed jacket.

1970, Japan, 13" x 13", cotton.
A man's handkerchief, soft and elegant, yet surprisingly thick and sturdy, not printed or overlaid in any way, but a true plaid. The combination of color and design is simple and remarkably balanced.

Top left:
Contrasting textures, silk and cotton flannel paired
with contrasting patterns, stripes and plaid, is a
daring but harmonious combination.

Top right:
An elegant silk hanky and casual brushed cotton sport
shirt announce an interesting person who is at home
in two different worlds.

TAMMIS KEEFE

"Color is the most important factor in design generally, and in handkerchief design specifically."

Keefe wrote those words in 1952, when she was the reigning queen of handkerchief designers in America. She was known for her deft combinations of colors—sage greens with pale pinks, grays with purples—and for her single-subject handkerchiefs—chairs, rabbits, owls, cats—the subject repeated several times on what she regarded as her "canvas."

Keefe thought of her designs as paintings, and her most avid fans framed her handkerchiefs, considering them genuine works of art. Keefe handkerchiefs purchased for fifty cents in the 1950s are worth a considerable amount more than that today if in good condition.

She also produced handkerchiefs under the pseudonym Peg Thomas, selling these equally cheerful hankies to merchants who wanted her fun and carefree look but couldn't afford to carry her signature line.

To think she got into handkerchief design by making a fanciful, boldly colorful handkerchief as a birthday gift for a friend! This friend showed it to a marketing person at Lord and Taylor's, he ordered a set of six designs, and they sold like hotcakes. A star was born and burned brightly until her death in 1960.

1950s, 16" x 15", silk.
An unusually controlled design for Tammis, but she lets loose and achieves beauty with her stunning color choices. This one is a favorite of both men and women.

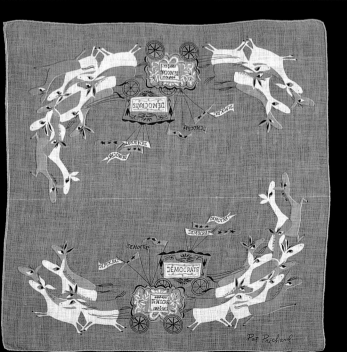

Top left:
1955, 14½" x 14½", cotton.
This is one of the most famous of all the Tammis Keefes. Cats were as popular fifty years ago as they are today, though no books had been published about why cats paint.

Top right:
1958, 15" x 14½", cotton.
It was inevitable that Tammis would employ the butterfly as a design element, echoing the classic Geisha motif, though her rendering is more matter-of-fact than sensual.

Bottom left:
1950s, 14½" x 14½", cotton.
Though not as well-known as Tammis Keefe, Pat Prichard was one of several designers who did very well in the 1950s and early 1960s with her Tammis-like creations. It may be unfair to say that Prichard copied Tammis's style, but there is no doubt that she benefited by the comparison.

1954, 13½" x 13", cotton.
All objects were fair game as design elements for Tammis. One wonders if she ever used handsaws or toilet bowls.
Probably.

CHILDREN'S HANDKERCHIEFS

Nursery rhymes, fairy tales, and favorite kiddy icons have long served as illustrations for children's hankies—generally smaller than Mom's, and made to be used.

Top right:
1940—60s, 8¾" x 8¾", cotton with appliquéd motif. A handmade sweetie-pie.

Bottom left:
1911, 12" x 12½", cotton.
A touching dedication written in a beautifully rounded Palmer Method handwriting: "For Leon from Grandma Kim P. Dec. 25, 1911." Firecrackers were a part of children's Christmas in the Old South at the turn of the century and onward. Very likely Leon was rewarded for behaving well, a common tradition and still in fashion in my childhood days until the 1950s. From the collection of Winifred and Phil Wood.

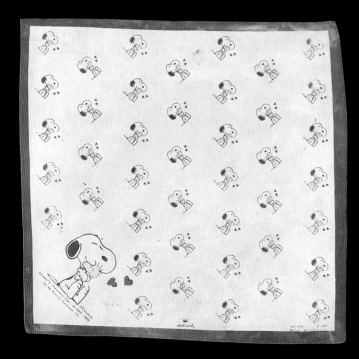

Top left:
1950s, 9½" x 9½", cotton.
A cute but lightweight everyday hanky. Machine hemmed.

Top right:
1940s, 8½" x 7½", cotton.
Clever topstitching on the central figures creates a pleasing illusion of movement. The tradition of placing Western icons in the four corners is carried out here.

Bottom left:
1980s, 12½" x 12½", cotton.
The young Josh Elwood took this hanky to countless baseball games. Now washed and ironed, it still bears the happy traces of ketchup, mustard, sweat, and grime. He required it; he never lost it, never left it behind. As a treasured object it is what I call a true handkerchief—an extension of the self. As in *Othello*, Desdemona's handkerchief *was* she, so in its own way this hanky was Josh.

$\mathscr{A}$N $\mathscr{U}$NBEATABLE
COLOR COMBINATION

$\mathscr{I}$f you want to catch someone's attention with a handkerchief, bring out an aqua-and-pink one. Cheap or expensive, it doesn't matter. I can't explain why this is such an appealing color combination, but having intentionally and unintentionally tested thousands of handkerchiefs on hundreds of people over the last sixty years, I can assure you that the combination of aqua and pink will always draw attention and admiration: "Now that's a beauty." Trust me on this one.

Her banner is a tear-stained hanky.

—Abigail Van Buren on melodramatic mothers-in-law

1940s, 12" x 12", cotton.
This ordinary machine-stitched hanky gets a comment whenever it is shown, ink stains and all.

SCHOOLGIRL HANKERCHIEFS

$\mathcal{M}$ost little girls worldwide between ages eight and thirteen tuck a brightly colored handkerchief into their pocket and go off to school. These handkerchiefs are usually plaids or sometimes solid colors. Usually machine hemmed, they are quite small and made to be used and lost. It is virtually impossible to tell what country these handkerchiefs come from, and it doesn't matter.

Such handkerchiefs are often wrapped around paper tubes and presented in boxes to give them a more substantial appearance. They are the often unimaginative, unwanted eighth-grade graduation gifts given by unpopular aunts or shirttail cousins. These handkerchiefs are not improved by ironing, they crumple immediately, and they rarely look clean—and nobody cares.

1955, France, 11" x 11¼", cotton.
A Confirmation gift belonging to my friend Marie Joseph. The "C" to the left of the larger initials is for Colette, who did all the embroidery in the small French village where "Mijo" spent her childhood.

1950, 12" x 12", cotton.
Small, inexpensive hankies were starched, folded, or rolled to make them look more substantial to the buyer. The blue hanky remains as it was purchased.

My Beatles Confession

In 1964, when I was a newly and happily married woman of thirty-four, the Beatles had recently landed in America and taken the country by storm. My husband and I watched their appearance on the *Ed Sullivan Show,* and we agreed that all those teenaged girls jumping up and down and screaming were stupid idiots. How I scorned them.

A month or so later, I found myself standing at the back of a huge auditorium filled with thousands of screaming girls—the Cow Palace in South San Francisco. I was heavily bedecked in scarves like some latter-day Scheherazade, so no one, especially any of my high school students, would recognize me.

I, too, was jumping up and down and screaming. The four mop tops looked like little dolls on that faraway stage and it was almost impossible to hear their music over the din of our communal wailing. I didn't care. I just joined the mystery of that fantastic rite of passage. There was, after all, safety in numbers.

1963, England, 15" x 15½", cotton. This Pop Art piece features very early song titles as well as a color and design style reminiscent of Tammis Keefe. The boys were already so well known in England that they no longer needed to be identified by name. From the collection of Winifred and Phil Wood.

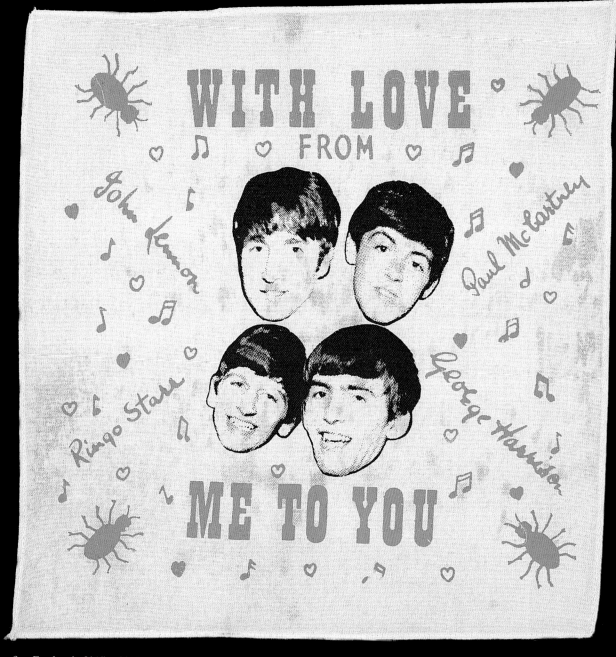

1963, England, 8½" x 8½", cotton.
Featuring replicas of the Beatles signatures, it is hard to imagine today that these clean-cut lads were considered shaggy-headed threats to American morality. This is also a very rare image of actual beetles in the same picture with the Beatles. The origin of their band name is much debated, though John Lennon once explained, "A man came down on a flaming pie and said, 'Let there be Beatles with an A.'" From the collection of Winifred and Phil Wood.

1920s, Armenian needle lace, 7¼" x 7¼", cotton, drawn work.
When this handkerchief came my way, I immediately identified it with Jackie Kennedy—elegant, restrained, and with a strong preference for the antique rather than the modern.

JACKIE KENNEDY

Around 1975, a friend of mine house-sat a penthouse apartment next door to Jackie Kennedy's flat on Fifth Avenue. From her bedroom window, my friend could look down and see a small part of Jackie's bathroom, including a section of the mirror above the sink. Late at night, she sometimes would see a light come on in Jackie's bathroom. She'd leap out of bed, hovering at the window, waiting and watching for a glimpse.

Every now and again, usually about a half hour after the light went on, two spidery thin hands would appear and place a limp piece of elegant white material on the mirror. Then these hands would smooth the fabric against the glass, squaring it perfectly. It was Jackie's handkerchief, and those were Jackie's hands.

"Ah," my friend said, "a real lady. She knows how to do it."

My mother and many other women would never think of putting their best handkerchiefs in a washing machine. Nor would they entrust them to their personal maids. A handkerchief of high quality was washed by the woman herself at the end of her day, using her finest facial soap. She would rinse it and smooth it into a square on a piece of glass, traditionally the bathroom vanity mirror. There it would cling until dry—usually overnight. The method was primitive but very effective. In the morning, "after the ball" the handkerchief was folded and put away in a handkerchief box or cedar-lined drawer. No ironing was necessary. It looked "ironed" as is.

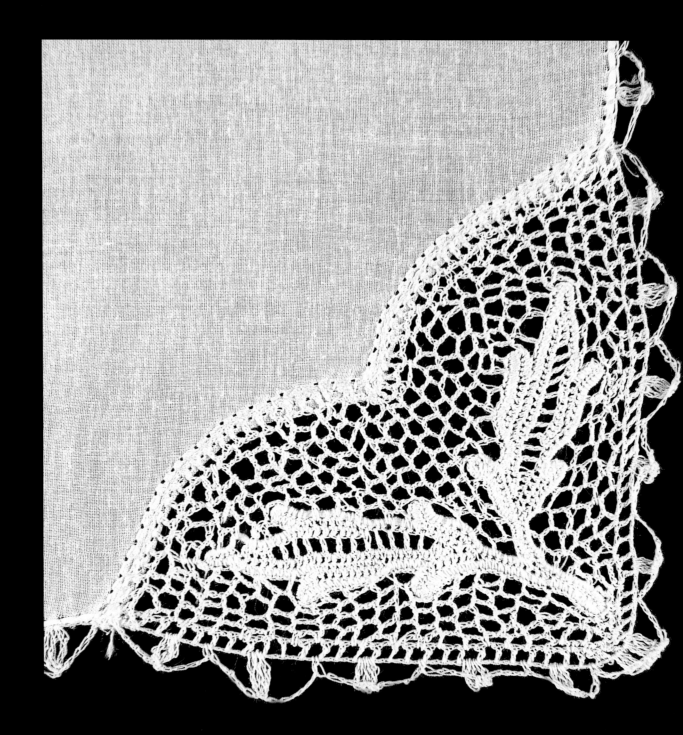

2000, 10½" x 11", cotton.
This lovely but inexpensive piece was displayed in the front window of the drugstore in Orvieto, Italy, and held in place by pins. The stitched leaf—a hasty rendering of the town symbol—was created by a local embroideress.

THE HISTORY
OF MY MANIA

My name is Helen, and I have a handkerchief problem. It all began innocently enough. When I was a little girl growing up in Minnesota in the 1930s, my mother made sure I had a clean hanky for school every day: a sturdy, utilitarian, plaid square of cotton cloth. I received prettier handkerchiefs as gifts throughout my childhood. It was never much of a problem to find handkerchiefs to match my various outfits. I could always borrow one from my mother in a pinch. I was extremely fashion conscious in my teens. I made many of my own clothes, as that was the only way I could keep pace with the most fashionable girls (the ones with money) at my school. I took handkerchiefs for granted then. They had to be right, of course, but I didn't spend much time worrying about them.

Then I went to college. This was in the late 1940s and early '50s. Handkerchiefs were all the rage, and I bought scads of them. All my girlfriends did, too. My top right dresser drawer, the shallow one known as the handkerchief drawer, was filled to bursting with pretty hankies. I must admit I was profligate with my horde. They were inexpensive and easy to find, so, yes, I lost them as we lose the throwaway pens of today.

At the height of my handkerchief mania, Kleenex completed its conquest of the American market. The handkerchief was accused by doctors and health officials of being a great repository for germs. By the late 1950s, handkerchiefs were not so easily bought. The huge displays of them in dime stores and department stores disappeared, and it was no longer considered gallant for a man to offer a woman in distress his handkerchief. Indeed, it was considered an assault on her health!

I took my habit underground, as did most of the women of my generation. We still gave and received handkerchiefs as gifts, but they had become more symbolic than usable—fabric greeting cards to be put away in the handkerchief box at the back of the closet. We wore scarves then, not handkerchiefs, even if some of those scarves really *were* handkerchiefs. Some men continued to wear handkerchiefs in their coat pockets, but only as one might wear a medal, as a kind of plumage.

Then in the early 1980s, my husband and I bought the old family farm in South Dakota, where we would spend our summers—a welcome respite from our busier lives in California. Along with the blissfully slow pace of life in South Dakota, and the lovely warm weather, I found myself in handkerchief heaven. The antique shops, estate sales, and garage sales were cornucopias of handkerchiefs. Exquisite pieces that now go for ten dollars or more as collectibles could be had for twenty-five cents. I tried to resist, but it was futile. My great longing to possess those gorgeous things was unleashed. I filled boxes with them, and feel immediately connected to each one, even a brand new purchase.

Sometimes when I close my eyes now, I see handkerchiefs floating down from the sky. I also see a little French child reaching for his security handkerchief, what the French call the *dou dou.* I see bandits in old movies robbing stagecoaches, their faces masked with black bandanas. I see martyrs and revolutionaries awaiting execution, their eyes shielded from their impending death by a brave white handkerchief. I see lovers using their handkerchiefs to flirt and entice, to send silent messages of devotion and desire. I see the groom removing the handkerchief from the wedding contract to signify his willingness to assume responsibility for his bride, and I see the newlyweds dancing their wedding dance, each holding one end of a handkerchief as symbol of the new bond between them.

And in a small village, in the twilight, I see a circle of children playing the ancient game of Drop the Handkerchief, their shouts filling the air as one child chases another around the outside of the circle. I do hope one of them remembers to take the handkerchief home. I hate losing handkerchiefs.

湖廣會館

HuGuang Guildhall

2001, China, 11" x 11", polyester.
Purchased by my daughter, this present day souvenir completes the hundred-year span of this book. Like the first hanky in this collection, it is small, mass-produced, and features a decoration in one corner, with the overall field left blank. Even the scalloped edges are the same. To quote Alphonse Karr: *Plus ça change, plus cést la même chose.* (The more things change, the more they remain the same.)

RESOURCES FOR HANDKERCHIEF FANCIERS

(A partial list of personal sources)

COLLECTIONS

Allentown Art Museum
Michele Boardman, *Curator of Textiles*
5th and Court Streets
P.O. Box 388
Allentown, PA 18105
www.allentownaartmuseum.org

The Billy Rose Theater Collection
The New York Public Library
    for the Performing Arts
40 Lincoln Center Plaza
New York, NY 10023
www.theatrediv@nypl.org

Bowers Museum
Santa Ana Textile Guild
2002 N. Main Street
Santa Ana, CA 92706
www.bowers.org

Cooper-Hewitt National Design Museum
2 East Ninety-first Street
New York, NY 10128
(212) 860-6868

Costume Society of America
55 Edgewater Drive
PO Box 73
Earleville, MD 21919
www.costumesocietyamerica.com

Fullerton Museum Center
301 N. Pomona Avenue
Fullerton, CA 92832
www.ci.fullerton.ca.us/museum/

Los Angeles County Museum of Art
Dale Gluckman, *Assistant Curator of Textiles*
5905 Wilshire Boulevard
Los Angeles, CA 90036
www.lacma.org

The Oakland Museum of California
Inez Brooks-Myers, Curator
1000 Oak Street
Oakland, CA 94607
www.museumca.org

EXPERTS

Elizabeth S. Brown
45 Whirlpool Way
Belle Meade, NJ 08502

Inez Brooks-Myers
The Oakland Museum of California
1000 Oak Street
Oakland, CA 94607
(510) 238-3842

Evelyn Kennedy
391 Long Hill Road
P.O. Box 1293
Groton, CT 06340
(860) 445-7320

Federation of Vintage Fashion
Vintage! (newsletter)
401 Dan Gabriel
Vallejo, CA 94590
(707) 793-0773

Gayle Wilson
c/o Fergeson Antique Mall
3742 Kellog Avenue
Cincinnati, OH 45226
(613) 321-7341

VENDORS

Ita Aber
2600 Netherland Avenue
Bronz, NY 10463-4815
(914) 968-4863

Lynne Wiener
William Doyle Auctioneers
50 King Street, 6F
New York, NY 10014
(212) 929-7108
By appointment

Sue Morse
Emma's Trunk
1701 Orange Treet Lane
Redlands, CA 92374
(909) 798-7865